Computer Software for Data Communications

Computer Software for Data Communications

William D. Skees

 LIFETIME LEARNING PUBLICATIONS ● Belmont, California
A Division of Wadsworth, Inc.

Designer: Michael A. Rogondino
Developmental Editing: Nancy Palmer Jones
Illustrator: John Foster

Printed in the United States of America

2 3 4 5 6 7 8 9 10—85 84 83 82 81

Library of Congress Cataloging in Publication Data
Skees, William D.   1939–
  Computer software for data communications.

  Includes bibliographical references and index.
  1.   Electronic digital computers—Programming.
2.   Computer networks.   I.   Title.
QA76.6.S597   001.64′2   80-24266
ISBN 0-534-97979-3

CONTENTS

PREFACE

The field of data communications influences the work of almost everyone in the computer world, and many programmers now feel the need to increase their knowledge and skills through familiarity with data communications systems. Although many books have been written to explain the hardware, networking, and protocols of these systems, this book is the first to answer the programmers' needs by dealing exclusively with the software of data communications.

Who Studies Communications Software?

This book will serve as a reference source for four main groups of computer professionals:

(1) Designers of a new data communications system

(2) Programmers assigned to modify an existing system

(3) Analysts who need to plan for and evaluate data communications systems

(4) Managers considering the procurement of a data communications system

Some systems designers will produce a communications system from scratch, operating system and all. Others will add data communications extensions to an existing application or to an operating system. This book identifies the components of data communications, explains the functions that such software must perform, and shows how the components are related to one another.

Programmers involved in developing or modifying the program code of a data communications system will need answers to questions such as these: What is different about data communications software? What are its various functions? What functions should be provided and how should they be organized? This book provides answers to these questions and others. It teaches programmers how to analyze and understand the structure of the system they are maintaining.

Analysts will need to understand how a data communications software system does its job, how it operates under fully or lightly loaded conditions, how its thoughtput can be measured and whether it can be improved. This book shows analysts how performance measurement capabilities can be included in the software.

Finally, procurement specialists will need to understand the inner workings of data communications software in order to answer such questions as: will a given vendor's system do the job? Will another system do it better? What is going on inside all that software? Will the code continue to operate with other equipment and under different workloads? This book provides the introduction to software concepts that the procurement specialist needs.

Is Previous Experience Necessary?

Readers of this book need some familiarity with such data communications hardware as keyboard terminals. I assume that their backgrounds will consist primarily of batch, with occasionally some online, applications because most programmers start off programming batch systems.

I also assume that programmers and designers who read this book will have a minimum of three years' experience on which to draw as they learn about data communications software. At the same time, managers and analysts who are not programming specialists will find the material up through Chapter 6 directly suited to their needs for a foundation in data communications software.

The Scope of This Book

This book provides an overview of current concepts in data communications software. It explains and compares various data communications systems from the point of view of communication objectives rather than concentrating on one particular application of the concepts. Thus, readers can use this book as a reference for a wide range of data communications systems.

By classifying and describing the data communications program functions, this book shows programmers that there is more to data communications software than simply data link control. Programmers and analysts trying to make sense out of published national and international standards will find here the information they need to translate those standards into software terms. And finally, this book serves as a guide for all those who are concerned about developing or selecting the data communications system which will best satisfy their particular needs.

1

Defining Data Communications Software and Its Importance

This chapter opens with a discussion of the importance of data communications software: its cost, visibility, and complexity. We then provide basic definitions for data communications and data communications software, and we describe its widespread use in the computer world. The final section of this chapter gives an overview of the structure of this book and of the topics that we will cover in the chapters to come.

The Importance of Data Communications Software

Cost   Computer center managers trying data communications for the first time and accustomed to monthly computer rental costs in five figures often find that the costs for telephone communications lines are even higher than their computer costs. A single dedicated line from Washington, D. C., to San Francisco, California, for example, can cost several thousand dollars per month.

Telephone lines are not the only communications-related costs in a data communications network. Some networks use hundreds of terminals, each costing a thousand dollars or more and all requiring maintenance. The additional hardware needed to make a communications computer out of the mainframe is expensive, and the costs of designing, programming, and testing communications software are even greater than the hardware costs.

Visibility   Not only the cost of data communications software but also its quality is highly visible within the corporation. Traditionally, a company would leave all its computing to employees in its computer center; now anybody in the company may have access to a data communications terminal. Thus the ups and downs, the throughputs and bottlenecks of an organization's computer network affect employees at every level of the corporate structure. Every success and every foulup may have top corporate visibility.

Complexity   As the number of data communications systems and their applications has increased, so has their complexity. Originally, communications networks supplied only remote batch services transmitting batch jobs to a central computer from remote card readers. Now these networks may support *message switching* (the delivery of messages from one terminal to another) and *online data entry* (the entry of information directly into the computer using a terminal instead of punched cards or paper tape). Programs that once used the straightforward transfer of disk or tape files over telephone lines, when elapsed time was not critical, are now being rewritten for real-time transmission, where not only elapsed time but also time of day are vital to successful execution. All of these changes in the complexity and flexibility of data communications systems reflect recent developments in communications software.

The cost, visibility, and complexity of data communications systems have made communications software experts essential to the efficient operation of an organization. Complex and costly systems need software that is carefully designed and carefully written. This book introduces the concepts that govern well-designed, well-written data communications software, and it describes the functions that all communications software must accomplish in order to work at all.

Basic Definitions

Data Communications   The term *data communications* means the use of computers to send digital information over communications facilities such as telephone lines, coaxial cables, and satellite networks. This definition emphasizes three important aspects of data communications. First, although some noncomputerized communications systems do exist, by tradition we reserve the term data communications for only those systems that use the computer for their decision-making, transmitting, and recording activities.

Second, the *data* must be *digital*. A network like that of the telephone company, which uses computers for switching voice signals, is not considered a data communications system. On the other hand, if the telephone company uses its computer switching network for the transmission of digitized voice information, then the resulting combination constitutes a data communications system.

Third, *communications facilities*, or facilities that provide communication between two or more locations, are required. The network must include a telephone line or its equivalent and may involve a long-distance link such as a microwave or satellite channel.

Data Communications Software   The term *data communications software* means the software that provides the functions of a system for data communications. While the computers in a data communications system may fulfill other tasks besides data communications, we are concerned only with the software that is directly involved with data communications. This includes software written specifically for control of communications hardware. Communications hardware control does overlap with such conventional operating system functions as interrupt handling and the execution of input/output commands, but only when the entire operating system is dedicated to communications functions may we consider the operating system to be a part of the data communications software.

Data communications software also includes the scheduling activities of message switching, but it usually does not include the very similar scheduling activities of a multiprogramming operating system. If, however, the communications system is engaged in either remote job entry or timesharing, then the scheduling activities of message handling and multiprogramming are very intricately related (see Chapter 9).

The word *software* in the definition refers not only to conventional software in random-access memory but also to microcode in read-only memories.

Where Data Communications Software Is Used Communications software is used throughout the spectrum of computer systems. It is found in the most modest of minicomputer systems where the console typewriter is hooked to the mainframe by a communications interface, and it is used when a full blown minicomputer becomes a remote terminal for a larger computer.

Large computer systems using data communications software range from those in a central service bureau that handle remote job entry customers to international computer networks that use distributed processing and that include a dozen or more different types of mainframes. Even computers that were installed with no thought of data communications requirements are being upgraded for the purposes of remote data collection. For instance, if a distant office is added to an organization or if new computer-aided graphics design demands a remote graphics terminal, then data communications software and hardware will be used to expand the existing computer system.

The widespread use of communications software has determined the organization of this book. Throughout the coming chapters we will discuss specific applications of communications software and how these applications affect the structure of the software.

The Structure of This Book

The natural approach to learning is through induction, moving from the description of specific instances and examples to the establishment of general ideas and principles. Thus, Chapter 2 introduces some of the more familiar uses of data communications software. General definitions are then developed from these frequently encountered software functions and packages.

Chapter 3 shows that data communications software is shaped by the organizational, industrial, mechanical, and procedural requirements of the user's environment. Chapter 4 then shows how logical constructs called protocols, which are implemented through software, meet the requirements identified in Chapter 3.

Chapter 5 deals very briefly with the hardware interface level of protocol. This material is included because the software expert must have some understanding of the hardware media through which the software operates and of the physical functions that it performs. The hardware section is brief, however, because there are many books on data communications to which the reader may turn for additional information. Some of these references are listed at the end of the chapter.

After the discussion of hardware protocols, we move on to higher level protocols. Chapter 6 deals with the practical problem of how code is organized physically and logically to support the protocols. This chapter also identifies the functions of software protocols and groups them on the basis of similar responsibilities. Chapters 7 and 8 explore each function in some detail.

Chapter 9 shows how the software functions support the traditional applications of data communications software. By this point the reader should have a sound knowledge of how the software of his or her particular application operates or may be expected to operate.

Chapter 10 then introduces the important concept that the "data" of data communications includes not only real or user data but also *metadata*, that is, data about data, about the data paths in the network, and about the operational status of the network. "Metacommunications" is on the frontier in the development of modern protocols.

Finally, Chapter 11 deals with the software functions necessary for keeping the data communications software itself operational. These functions are further examples of metacommunications and are the current focus of interest for programmers in the field of data communications software.

2

Familiar Kinds of Data Communications Software

In order to establish a frame of reference that will be useful throughout the remainder of the text, this chapter defines five of the most frequently encountered kinds of data communications software: data link control, telecommunications access methods, communications packages and turnkey systems, and network architectures.

Data Link Control (Device and Line Handlers)

Data link control, hereafter referred to as DLC, is the software that transmits and receives data over a communications line and that monitors this transmission and receipt for error recovery purposes. Since data communications transmission is normally bit serial (that is, data is transmitted one bit at a time) and since remote transmission media are much less reliable than local data channels (one error per 1,000 bits of data as opposed to one per 10,000,000), DLC is much more complicated than conventional computer center input/output software.

Conventional computer center input/output software modules are called *I/O handlers*; they control local data channels, hardware controllers, and such local devices as card readers, tape drives, and disks. The I/O handlers operate in *bit parallel* mode (eight to thirty-two bits at a time) over distances of fifty feet or less. Normally, these batch handlers deal only with solicited interrupts, such as the interrupt that follows a tape rewind command. Some locally connected peripherals such as console typewriters do generate unsolicited interrupts (that is, interrupts not specifically requested by the system), but these are usually handled by the software techniques of data link control.

DLC also controls remote terminals and other computers. But, unlike conventional input/output software, DLC does not communicate directly with the device, or even with the hardware controller of the device, to which it is reading or writing. DLC does manipulate a controller, but it is a *communications controller* that is connected to a telephone line adaptor or its equivalent; this adaptor is, in turn, connected to a modem. (A *modem* or *modulator/demodulator*, is the hardware that converts digital signals from the computer into analog signals for the telephone line.) Figure 2-1 shows the relationship of DLC software to the communications controller and the remote device.

The line adaptor, shown in Figure 2-1, is a kind of specialized plug. Its generic term is *hardware* (or communications) *interface*. There is almost always a modem in the chain between the communications controller and the remote device, even for communications facilities that are entirely digital. Such facilities require a modem in order to make the signal conversions necessary for the communications media. The distinction between modulating to analog media and modulating to digital media is not usually of concern to the software programmer.

The Elements of the Controller The ultimate function of data link control is to control the electronic pulses on the connector

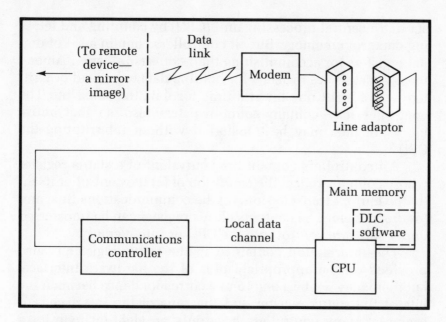

FIGURE 2-1. Relationship of DLC to Communications Controller and Remote Device

pins in the hardware interface. One of the pins, for example, may be used for timing, another for showing computer or terminal on/off status, another for transmitting or receiving data, and so on. But, although it is the function of DLC to set or to sense pin signals, most controllers relieve DLC of the need to do so directly.

If DLC were to work directly at the pin level, DLC software would have to control the individual bits of each data item while at the same time sensing other status and timing bits and turning them on and off as necessary. Generally speaking, hardware is much better at such simultaneous activities than is software. Thus, DLC and the controller work together in a kind of hierarchy: the software issues read and write commands and identifies or supplies data to be transmitted; the controller converts read and write commands into sequences of pin settings and makes the conversion between data words or bytes and data bits.

Controller capabilities vary from the simplest conversion functions to more sophisticated operations. Some controllers act like a central processing unit *(CPU)* by counting and fetching data from memory. But all controllers contain a set of digital registers for accomplishing their conversion tasks. Among these registers are registers for holding data to be read or written, which shift one bit at a time for data transmission. The controller may contain count registers also, so that entire blocks of data may be transferred without interrupting the CPU.

All controllers contain the equivalent of a status register whose contents reflect the condition of (a) the controller itself, (b) the current transmission, (c) the communications line, and (d) the modem. The contents of this register can be transferred under software control into the CPU or into memory.

The information contained in the status register is also provided on the appropriate pins of the hardware interface, but there may not be a one-to-one correspondence between the bits of the status register and the pins of the interface. For example, many controllers have only an eight-bit byte for a status register, but they use the 25-pin RS-232C interface, which is a standard interface in the United States for low- to medium-speed transmission. The correspondence between these pin settings and the representations in the status register can only be figured out based on the controller's technical specifications. If the programmer is debugging DLC code and needs to read the pins of the interface directly, there are dozens of communications test devices on the market. These devices are actually calculators with communications probes that attach to the interface. The calculators contain microprograms of various degrees of sophistication.

A Sample Transmission   In order to achieve an output transmission through the controller, DLC first issues a command such as a WRITE DIRECT to select the particular telephone line or port (where the line enters the controller) that the controller is to use. This process is analogous to the selection of a tape drive on a magnetic tape channel, with one difference. On a tape controller we use the address of the tape drive or its position on the channel, which is one and the same with the address of the device. On a communications controller we use the address of the line or port over which we intend to communicate. The actual device address is not used at this stage. There may be more than one device on the line, each with its own address. We will see later that the particular device address is a datum in the message that we send, but it is not a part of the physical I/O instruction.

Next, DLC tells the controller to begin transmitting from location A in memory and to count n bytes or words. This is usually accomplished by loading the controller's memory-address register with A and its count register with n and then issuing the command WRITE.

In a *direct memory access (DMA)* system, where the controller can reach directly into memory for each of the bytes to be transmitted, the controller usually proceeds without bothering the CPU until all data have been transmitted for that particular line. The controller then generates an interrupt that the operating system will hand over to DLC. Data link control will issue interrogating commands or proceed to interpret certain memory registers in order to find out which communication has completed and whether it was input or output. Such analysis is necessary in DLC because the communications controller is a *multiplexed device*—that is, the controller is capable of handling several transmissions simultaneously. Obviously, DLC must be designed to operate under conditions of simultaneity and to take maximum advantage of the ability of the controller to do many things at once.

After determining which line is involved, DLC interrogates the status register of the controller or the CPU, or it looks at a particular location in memory, depending on the hardware architecture. This enables DLC to find out (a) whether the transmission was completed, (b) whether any errors were detected, and (c) whether the equipment involved was still operational at the end of the transmission.

The reader should note that, in this description of a transmission intended for a target device such as a terminal or another computer, we do not mention either reading or writing on that device itself. Data link control's perception of what has happened at the device is limited to what it can learn from the interface. Whether a remote device actually received the communication, or was even operational during the period of transmission, is not conveyed directly to DLC. Instead, DLC must deduce these facts from the context within which interrupts occur, and from the status and data registers that it reads from the controller. DLC never reads directly from a remote device; it only reads the contents of the controller's data registers.

For instance, if an input interrupt occurs when expected, it is a partial indication of a good input transmission. DLC then checks the status and data registers to complete the validation. If no input occurs or if an unexpected interrupt occurs, then there is a problem either on the line, at the other end, or in the message-level dialogue.

From the status and data registers DLC learns whether the message went out of the controller in good shape or in bad shape. All an error indication tells DLC, however, is that an error existed somewhere in the transmission or in the error indicator itself. Similarly, lack of an error indication may mean a good transmission, or it may mean that the error mechanism failed. The point is that DLC is dependent on the controller for information about the transmission, and the information DLC receives is indicative, not definitive.

Telecommunications Access Methods

A *telecommunications access method* is a vendor-supplied data link control with a software interface such as a Fortran, COBOL, PL/1, or assembly-language subroutine call linkage. Figure 2-2 shows these components. The subroutine call capability makes it possible for an application to use data link control without requiring the applications programmer to know very much about data communications details.

IBM, as an example of one vendor and the first to use the phrase "access method" across its I/O product line, offers a hierarchy of telecommunications access methods. All of them represent extensions to its Basic Telecommunications Access Method, called BTAM, which was introduced in the mid-1960s for its System 360 computers. QTAM, for instance, is a BTAM

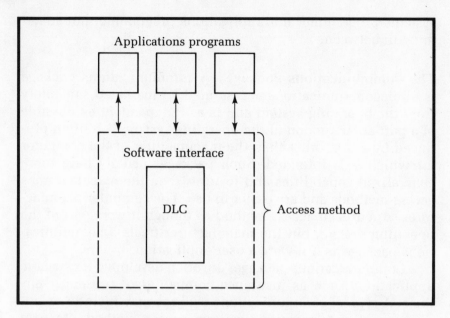

FIGURE 2-2. Components of a Telecommunications Access Method

extension that provides automatic queueing of messages. Two other extensions provide a software interface to newer and more elaborate options in scheduling facilities in the operating system: TCAM services the timesharing option, and VTAM interfaces with the virtual storage option.

A telecommunications access method has a very intimate relationship with the operating system. The access method, for example, is permitted to use privileged instructions and to do its own interrupt handling. Since access methods have some features that resemble the operating system and since they usually are supported by the hardware vendor and may use the vendor's specialized updating procedures, telecommunications access methods are usually installed and maintained by a computer center's systems programmers, not by the applications programmer. However, since telecommunications access methods are also at the heart of a network application, programmers who need to develop effective network applications frequently become telecommunications access method specialists. They occupy a special job category that is neither systems programmer nor applications programmer but something in between.

The Communications Package A *communications package* is a telecommunications access method marketed separately from the operating system and is as independent as possible of a particular version of the operating system. It is often produced by a firm other than the manufacturer of the computer for which it is intended. Such packages usually have more generalized capabilities and features than the manufacturer's access methods and are easier to use. The computer manufacturer supports an access method as though it were part of the operating system, but the manufacturer treats a communications package as if it were a user application.

Communications packages are often developed for specific applications such as insurance companies or passenger airlines. A typical communications package may include, in addition to the telecommunications access method, its own scheduler for multiprogrammed functions, its own loader, and a disk input/output handler with its own data base management facility.

The Turnkey System A *turnkey system* is a communications package that occupies a dedicated computer. Turnkey systems are usually maintained by the vendor. They are used most frequently in message switching applications where they convert the computer they occupy into a communications processor. In these cases the computer is usually a minicomputer.

Some turnkey systems, however, do require larger computers because they are designed for big systems usage, such as large-scale data acquisition. Certain types of transaction-processing systems, such as theater reservations and off-track betting, may also use a dedicated turnkey system on a large computer.

For the systems designer, communications packages and turnkey systems have the important advantage of being available at a known cost. They are easy to evaluate for suitability to the application and, best of all, they are not subject to the scheduling and quality assurance problems of software developed in-house.

Network Architectures

The most glamorous term and, at present, possibly the most important term for the future development of software standards is *network architecture*. Network architecture means the design philosophy, and the implemented logical structure, of data communications software within a given hardware network framework. The term was popularized in the late 1960s by the creators of the ARPAnet, an international packet switching network developed under the sponsorship of the Advanced Research Projects Agency of the U. S. Department of Defense.

The Purposes of Network Architecture The word *network* can apply to any computer combination from the most modest configuration of a single computer and one remote card reader on the campus of a small college to the most imaginatively interconnected collection of mainframes and terminals used with multinational linkups. The word *architecture* indicates that the software is designed to optimize some of the following features:

- Network throughput—how much traffic can the network handle effectively?

- CPU utilization—how heavily and how effectively are the mainframes utilized?

- Cost recovery—how rapidly and how successfully does the network recover total hardware and software investment?

- Reliability—how well does the network do its job? (Reliability encompasses the network's accuracy, repeatability, error sensitivity, and recovery abilities.)

- Device compatibility—to what extent can unlike devices be accommodated?

- Ease of use—how easily can applications be adapted to the network and make use of the network's facilities?

- Ease of hardware reconfiguration—how easily and effectively can the hardware configuration be modified?

- Interface between software entities such as programs and data bases—what facilities exist for communication among programs?

Network Architecture and Data Communications Standards
Network architecture, then, means both (1) the written document that describes a philosophy and the rules for implementing its logic and (2) the implemented version of that philosophy. Because a network architecture is a software *concept*, it may be said that network architectures are developed by standards organizations, which perform no software development of their own. Because a network architecture is also defined by its *implementation*, it may be said that manufacturers and software houses also develop network architectures. Occasionally a large manufacturer, such as IBM among large-scale users or DEC among small-scale users, develops an architecture at the philosophical stage; these architectures tend to become de facto standards because of the manufacturer's economic impact on the field.

Often the communications software developed and installed at a particular computer center becomes a network architecture in its own right, exerting a strong influence on the selection and implementation of future applications within the organization. In other words, it too becomes a de facto standard, and future systems of that computer center use it as a baseline. To counteract these tendencies, there is a strong international interest in standardization. Through the efforts of standards organizations, the philosophy and rules for data communications software are becoming more formalized; the structure of messages, for example, and the relationships among levels of protocol and between data bases within and between data communications systems are being worked out for the systems of the future.

SUMMARY

This chapter has divided data communications software according to the form in which the software may be encountered by the programmer:

- Data link control—the software that controls the basic functions of the communications interface, usually coded directly in assembly language

- Access method—more elaborate software capabilities supplied by a manufacturer, which include data link control as a subset, usually invoked by assembly language macros

- Communications package—a complete data communications subsystem, usually easier to use than access methods and invoked by high level subroutine calls

- Turnkey system—a communications package installed by a vendor and tailored to a particular application, occasionally containing all the software required to run the application; a turnkey system may require a dedicated computer

- Network architecture—a concept or philosophy of software organization and procedures; also, the software in an existing network that includes both data link control and network functions

REFERENCES

Documentation Practices

Rubin, Martin L., ed. *Documentation Standards and Procedures for Online Systems.* New York: Van Nostrand Reinhold, 1979.

Fundamentals of Data Communications

Doll, Dixon R. *Data Communications—Facilities, Networks, and Systems Design.* New York: John Wiley and Sons, 1978.

Martin, James. *Systems Analysis for Data Transmission.* Englewood Cliffs, N. J.: Prentice-Hall, 1972

Martin, James. *Telecommunications and the Computer.* 2nd ed. Englewood Cliffs, N.J.: Prentice-Hall, 1976.

Microdata Corporation. *The Communications Handbook.* Irvine, Calif., 1973.

Sippl, Charles J. *Data Communications Dictionary.* New York: Van Nostrand Reinhold, 1976.

Hardware Interface

Electronics Industries Association. "Interface between Data Terminal

Equipment and Data Communications Equipment Employing Serial Binary Data Interchange." EIA RS-232C. Washington, D. C., 1969.

IBM Telecommunications Access Methods
See the following IBM sources:
    (1) TCAM—IBM Reference Manuals GC30-2022 and GC30-2024
    (2) VTAM—IBM Reference Manuals GX27-0024 and GV-8225

I/O Handlers
Madnick, Stuart E., and Donovan, John J. *Operating Systems.* New York: McGraw-Hill, 1974.

Modems
Green, Paul E., Jr. "Computer Communications." IEEE reprint, 1974.

Network Architectures
Davies, Donald W., and Barber, Derek L. A. *Communications Networks for Computers.* New York: John Wiley and Sons, 1973.

Donaldson, Hamish. *Designing a Distributed Processing System.* New York: John Wiley and Sons, 1979.

Martin, James. *Communications Satellite Systems.* Englewood Cliffs, N. J.: Prentice-Hall, 1978.

Weitzman, Cay. *Distributed Micro/Minicomputer Systems.* Englewood Cliffs, N. J.: Prentice-Hall, 1980.

For further information about network standards, the reader may refer to publications of the American National Standards Institute (ANSI), the Consultative Committee for International Telephony and Telegraphy (CCITT), the International Organization for Standardization (ISO), the Electronics Industries Association (EIA), and the Federal Telecommunications Standards Committee (FTSC). Most of the standards with which this text is concerned are reproduced in McGraw-Hill's *Data Communications Standards*.

3

The Objectives of Data Communications Software

To understand data communications software, the programmer must first know why it is written. In this chapter, we examine the following objectives of data communications software:

- Communication between devices

- Communication between users, or between users and applications

- Communication between data bases

- Communication between applications

- Management and control of communications activities

This chapter shows how these objectives differ from one another and what problems arise when we try to implement systems to meet these objectives. The subsequent chapters show how these objectives are met.

Device-Oriented Communications

Types of Transmission   Probably the most common objective in data communications systems is simply that of getting devices to talk to one another. This means that device A can send a datum x to device B and that device B will recognize the datum as x and will work with it, in context. Figure 3-1 shows this relationship in its simplest form.

The qualification *in context* is essential. For example, device A will always want device B to recognize datum x as, say, the number 6, but device A may sometimes want device B to print the character 6 and at other times to treat the 6 as the count of all records that have been transmitted to date between A and B. Figure 3-2 illustrates the transmission of character 6 in a print context, and Figure 3-3 shows the number 6 as a sequence number.

In Figure 3-2, device A is transmitting the character 6, which is to be printed on a printer or reproduced (*displayed*) on a video display device. In this case, the character 6 signifies itself. The transmission is typical of character-oriented communication in the asynchronous mode—that is, one character is transmitted at a time. ASCII is a national standard code for character representation (see Chapter 7).

In Figure 3-3, a video display, which is capable of displaying many characters simultaneously, is transmitting information to another device with similar capabilities. Frequently such devices are also capable of transmitting several characters

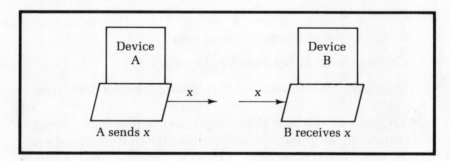

FIGURE 3-1.   Communication between Devices

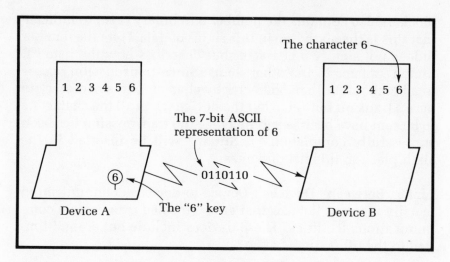

FIGURE 3-2.   The Numbers Transmitted in a Print Context

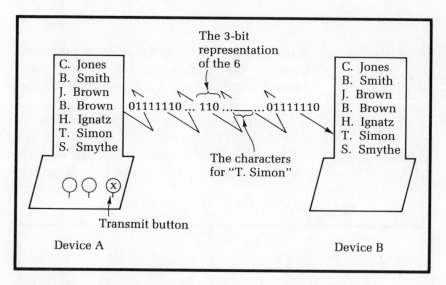

FIGURE 3-3.   The Number 6 Transmitted as a Sequence Number

as a block. This is called *synchronous transmission*. This example shows a single line of the display being transmitted. The block contains the *signal* (or *framing*) bit pattern of IBM's SDLC (01111110) used to delineate the beginning and ending of this block. It also contains the number 6 in binary (110) to indicate that this is the sixth line in this series of data. Here the number 6 does not signify a character but describes how the data "T. Simon" relates to the other items. Since transmission occurs in a block rather than character by character, it is necessary to have a transmit button to tell the device when all the characters to be sent have been keyed in. Once the transmission has been successfully completed, "T. Simon" will be inserted in the sixth place in this list of names.

Links Between Devices Device-to-device communication usually involves devices that are connected over remote communications facilities. These devices include but are not limited to the following:

- Two keyboard terminals
- A terminal of any sort and a computer
- Two computers

For our purposes, a programmable terminal falls in the category with *terminals* rather than computers if it is under user (as opposed to program) control and if the application for which it is employed resides elsewhere.

The devices may be connected over a single data link or over several data links through intermediate computers, as illustrated in Figures 3-4 and 3-5. For software purposes we may think of a *single data link* as being a telephone line. It makes

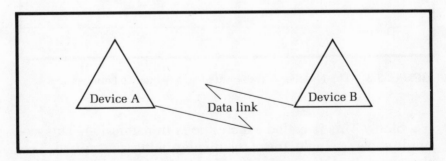

FIGURE 3-4. Two Devices Connected over a Single Data Link

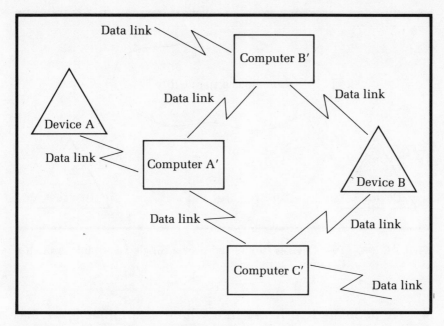

FIGURE 3-5. Two Devices Connected over Several Data Links through Intermediate Computers

no difference whether this telephone line goes directly from one device to the other or goes through a myriad of telephone offices and switching centers. They are all the same to data communications software. It also makes no difference to the software whether the data-link facility is provided by the telephone company, by a specialized carrier (such as Microwave Communications, Incorporated—MCI) or by a combination of both.

Whether or not the facility supplier (who is called the *common carrier*) utilizes computers of its own along the data link is immaterial to data communications software. Figure 3-6 indicates that the software cannot "see" the inner workings of the common carrier. In other words, if device A is in San Francisco and device B is in New York, they are unaffected by the presence or absence of any telephone company computers that may be active between them. What does matter is how the data link looks to the device. That is, the software may treat the data link as one or another of the following:

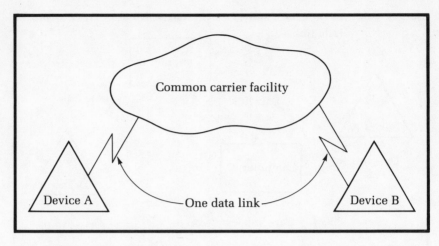

FIGURE 3-6. Two Devices Connected over a Single Data Link through a Common Carrier

- A *dedicated* (*private*) line where a terminal is permanently connected at each end

- A *dial-up* line where one terminal dials the other over a switched network

- A *multidrop* line where several terminals are permanently connected on the same line

Devices may also be connected over *several data links* through intermediate computers. In this case the data communications software is very much concerned with the intermediate computers. We refer to this configuration as a *data communications network*, and it is illustrated in Figure 3-7. Devices A and B are again located in San Francisco and New York, but here they are a part of a network belonging to a large company such as General Motors, and they are hooked up to General Motors computers in Michigan, Texas, and Tennessee, for instance. Telephone company facilities connect all of these devices, but any message from device A to device B must also go through two General Motors computers along the way. Such a network may consist solely of its terminals, its intermediate computers, and its private data links. Most networks, however, use common carrier facilities.

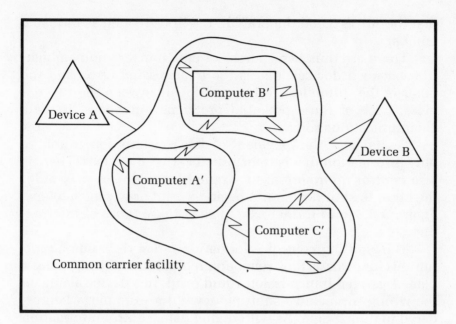

FIGURE 3-7. Two Devices Connected by a Data Communications Network Using Common Carrier Facilities

Problems in Device-Oriented Communications One of the problems faced by device-oriented communications is that the existence of a data link between two devices implies that there will be frequent transmission errors. Yet the applications software that runs on the two devices requires that the transmission be unambiguous. The transmitted number 6, for example, must always be recognized by the receiver as a 6, regardless of the context. The number 7 would not be an acceptable substitute.

Another potential problem is that each of the two devices may represent the number 6 as a different binary pattern in its memory. For example, one terminal may represent the number in the American National Standard Code for Information Interchange, or ASCII as 011 0110, while a terminal that uses IBM's Extended Binary Coded Decimal Interchange Code (EBCDIC) will express the number 6 as 1111 0110. Since the storage patterns are different, either the sending terminal or the receiving terminal must make an internal conversion so that the ASCII 6 and the EBCDIC 6 will be treated as the same number.

There are thus two sources of data transmission ambiguities between devices: one is the transmission error, and the other is the difference in internal logic between the two devices. Each of these potential problems influences the data communications software.

Digital data, the "payload" of data transmission, is not the only information that is transmitted between devices. There is also *control information*; for example, one device may order the other to shut down or to begin to print or to punch a tape. Figure 3-8 shows further examples of these types of information.

Transmitting control information offers the same opportunities for error as those encountered in transmitting payload data. A garbled transmission could result in a device acting on the wrong command—shutting down, for example, when ordered to punch tape. As with digital data, control information

	Payload Data	Control Information
Between keyboard terminals	Display (print) data Nondisplay (secure) data	Carriage return New line/New page Device on/off Error check sequence Mechanical status
Between a terminal and a computer	Display and nondisplay data Data records (e.g., card images, portions of files)	All of the above plus: Message count End of transmission
Between two computers	All of the above	All of the above plus: Processor status

FIGURE 3-8. Device-Oriented Payload Data and Control Information

must be converted into an internal code appropriate to the device involved; a conversion failure may also result in misinterpretation of a command.

Control code discrepancies are part of the larger problem of the lack of standardization in data communications. I recall a system implemented on a timesharing network where the vendor assured my client that only the "break" signal would interrupt transmission. We found by experimentation that, contrary to the vendor's assurance, a binary pattern equivalent to the EOT (end of transmission) character (bit pattern 0011 0111 in EBCDIC and 000 0100 in ASCII) would not only interrupt the transmission but would also initiate an "answer back" response from the network that would very effectively obliterate whatever else we were trying to send.

Finally, device-to-device communications must ensure electromechanical compatibility between the two devices. For example, the faster terminal must slow down to the speed of the other terminal, or else a buffer must be added so that the slower terminal can retain data that it receives at high speed until it is able to dispose of the data properly.

To summarize, in order to achieve device-to-device communication we must accomplish the following with data communications software:

- Select and maintain a communications route between devices across data links that are under control of the communications network

- Recognize and resolve transmission errors

- Resolve internal logic differences between each pair of devices

- Identify and resolve device control discrepancies

- Simulate electromechanical compatibility between dissimilar devices

User-Oriented Communications

The next most common objective for data communications software is that of permitting *users*—human beings using the computer facilities—to communicate with one another or with applications programs running in remote computers.

The user, like the terminal device, works with two types of transmission—payload data and control information. The user transmits payload data when he or she credits a dollar amount to an account in a banking application, for example. The user transmits control information when he or she instructs the computer to stop a program that is part of an application or when he or she signals an intention to end a session at the terminal. Figure 3-9 shows examples of user-oriented payload data and control information.

Both types of information are contained in messages that the user enters onto the data link from a terminal. To render the context of the data unambiguous and to make the user's time at the terminal both efficient and productive, elaborate rules for user dialogue have been developed for every user-oriented system. These constitute a special level of protocol that we will discuss in Chapter 8.

In order to achieve user-to-user or user-to-application communication, the data communications software must make it possible to do the following:

- Identify and contact the target user or application—for example, process the command to select a particular terminal or a particular program

- Exchange payload data and control information with the

Payload Data	Control Information
Text	Logon/Logoff
Numbers	Application selection
Queries	Application start/stop
Responses	Interrupt
Records (card images, line images)	

FIGURE 3-9. User-Oriented Payload Data and Control Information

user or application—for example, transmit a message to that terminal or provide an input to that program

- Recognize and resolve logical errors in dialogue—for example, reject misspelled commands or reject input to an unidentified program.

Data-Oriented Communications

Data-oriented systems—or systems that are used as data resources—have only recently become popular. In fact, it is only recently that *data bases*—highly structured and usually large files of data—have been recognized as distinct entities of computer science and as fit objects for support by computer systems and computer networks.

Types of Data-Oriented Systems Since totally centralized data bases are not always feasible or even desirable, we now find two types of data-oriented systems: (1) systems representing a single data base distributed over a large geographical area and connected by data communications facilities (Figure 3-10) and (2) systems connecting several different data bases maintained in separate locations (Figure 3-11). Figure 3-10 shows a network that contains a single data base distributed geographically. The one data base is divided into six parts, according to the primary data needs of each locality—research in California, personnel in Chicago, marketing in Dallas, finance in New York, and so on. Each part of the data base is available to all other centers via communication lines and specialized data communications software.

Figure 3-11 shows several data bases connected through a common network. There are five plants; each has its own complete data base supporting its own needs. Each data base is available to the other sites for comparison, for analysis, for planning, and for development of composite corporate statistics. Because communication is so expensive, this approach is an economic optimum—it keeps the routine transactions local. It also permits identical software to be used at each site, thus reducing software development costs.

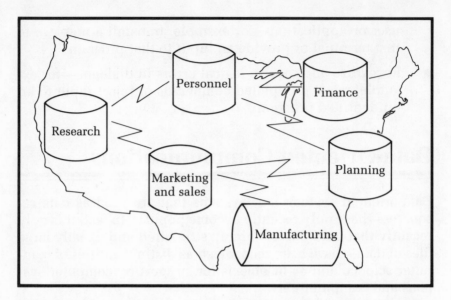

FIGURE 3-10. A Single Corporate Data Base Distributed Geographically

Whatever the logical separation of data, all data-oriented communications systems have two characteristics in common:

- They represent one or more data structures that are connected over communications media.

- Most of the work performed in the communications system consists of moving data back and forth.

Figure 3-12 gives examples of the types of data transmitted in a data-oriented system.

Applications-Oriented Communications

Somewhat more rare than device-, user-, or data-oriented communications systems are those that are set up to connect applications programs with one another. These systems permit programs to communicate directly with one another without

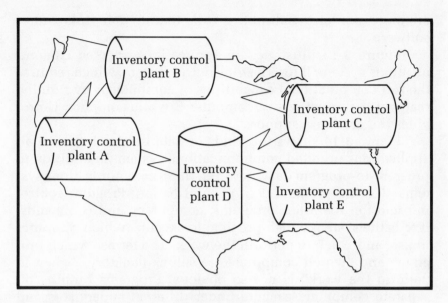

FIGURE 3-11. Several Data Bases Linked from Separate Locations

the intermediate action of a human being to analyze, interpret, codify, or modify inputs and outputs.

Intellectually it is a simple step from the concept of a data base as an entity in itself, independent of the computer or computers where it resides, to the concept of a program or set of programs operating as a logical entity independent of the host computers. The interconnections among these programs

Payload Data	Control Information
Numbers	Data base identification
Text	File identification
Records	Record identification
File segments	Item identification
Files	File copy start/stop
	Interrupts

FIGURE 3-12. Data-Oriented Payload Data and Control Information

are more similar to subroutine calls than to data link control software.

Figure 3-13 illustrates an applications-oriented communications system. It tests a ship control system, which requires the full computational capabilities of computer A by running real-world simulations in computer B while computer C provides the data base support.

Figure 3-14 shows the kinds of data involved in such an applications-oriented communications system. In addition to program-to-program data, however, these communications systems also use program control information. *Program control information* identifies programs, computers, and commands. It tells the system which program to execute, which computer to use, and when to perform the work. The terms "which program" and "which computer" are self-explanatory; "when to perform the work" is not so obvious. Programs running on separate computers execute under different supervisors and use different internal clocks. Since the programs operate on different machines and at different speeds, they cannot actually operate in "real time." Program control information

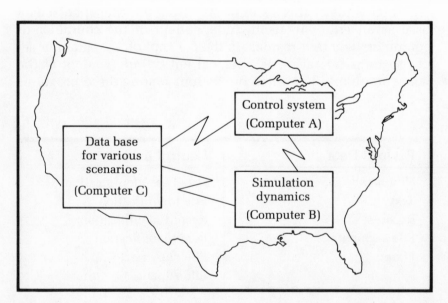

FIGURE 3-13. Applications-Oriented Communications—Ship Control System

Program-to-Program Payload Data	Program Control Information
Numbers	Applications identification
Text	Data base identification
Records	Applications start/stop
Inquiries	Interval/cycle/quanta timing
Responses	Interrupt

FIGURE 3-14. Applications-Oriented Payload Data and Control Information

causes programs to operate in relative time—based on priority, for instance—and thus to simulate real-time operation.

Network-Oriented Communications

The communication of information for network control purposes has recently become a system design objective in its own right. Large scale networks with thousands of terminals or with hundreds of computer processors need management and coordination in much the same way that large teams of human beings do. Network control provides that management and coordination.

Network control functions much like operating-systems control; it allocates common resources, for instance, when a problem can be solved by increasing the available resources, as in the processing of job streams in a computer service bureau network. Through this kind of resource management, network control allows the system to deal with the inevitable problems that occur when some computers are saturated, inoperative, or off-line, or when the data links are similarly not available or not completely responsive. In other words, a network-oriented communications system calls not only for sending payload messages from one location to another but also for sending "messages" which describe, query, modify, or re-establish network conditions. Figure 3-15 shows examples of the information transferred in network-oriented communications.

Payload Data	Control Information
Processor status	Computer identification
Line status	Communications processor
Message queue status	identification
Acknowledgment	Computer stop/start
Inquiry	

FIGURE 3-15. Network-Oriented Payload Data and Control Information

Figure 3-16 gives a diagram of the most widely known network-oriented communications system—the ARPAnet. The ARPAnet is a host-sharing system—the network software is oblivious to the individual applications programs that it supports; instead, its facilities permit each "host," or main computer, to talk to any other host in the network. Individual messages are handled as packets of a uniform size. The network control software resides in the switching computers, or Interface Message Processors (IMP's), which look at the source and destination of the message but not at its contents.

SUMMARY

Communications systems are developed in many different ways, following many different philosophies, subject to constraints that affect different systems in different ways. In order to make sense out of the various approaches that are used, we take the time in this chapter to step back and take a look at the most basic communications objectives:

● Device-to-device communication

● User-to-device communication

● User-to-application communication

● Application-to-application communication

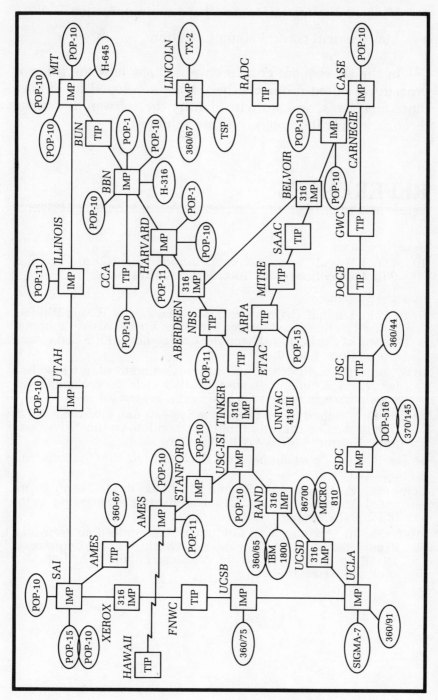

FIGURE 3-16. Example of a Network-Oriented Communications System— ARPAnet

- User- or application-to-data-base communication

- Management control communication

In the subsequent chapters we will see how the rules of procedure, called protocols, have been developed to address these objectives, and we will identify the software functions through which these objectives are achieved.

REFERENCES

Data Structures

Tremblay, J. P., and Sorenson, P. G. *An Introduction to Data Structures with Applications.* New York: McGraw-Hill, 1976.

Existing Systems

Heart, F. E., Kahn, R. E. Ornstein, S. M., Crowther, W. R., and Walden, D. C. "The Interface Message Processor for the ARPA Computer Network." Spring Joint Computer Conference: AFIPS Conference Proceedings, vol. 40, 1972.

IBM Corporation. *IBM 3705 Advanced Communications Function for NCP/VS Generation and Utilities Reference Manual.* Research Triangle Park, N.C.: IBM Corp., September 1978.

Logica, Ltd. "Report to the Computer Systems and Electronics Division of the Department of Industry, London, on the ARPA Computer Network." NTIS #AD/A-002 346, 1974.

McFayden et al. "Systems Network Architecture." *IBM Systems Journal,* 15 (1976): 4–80.

Schwartz, M., Boorstyn, R. R., and Pickholtz, R. L. "Terminal-Oriented Computer-Communications Networks." *Proceedings of the IEEE* 60 (November 1972).

Wolf, Eric W. "An Advanced Computer Communications Network." Paper read at AIAA Computer Network Systems Conference, 16–18 April 1973, Huntsville, Alabama. Published by Bolt, Beranek and Newman, Inc.

4

Meeting the Objectives—Data Communications Protocols

This chapter introduces the concept of data communications protocols, the means by which the objectives discussed in Chapter 3 are met. Data communications protocols are grouped in levels based on the functions they address. In this chapter, we give a brief definition of each level; the following chapters will discuss protocols in greater detail.

Definitions and Standards

A *protocol* is a formal set of rules by which two entities communicate with one another. Two devices must obey a common set of rules in transmitting data. Otherwise, the bit patterns that one transmits will look like *noise* (random, nontranslatable data) to the other. Rules are likewise necessary for dialogue between the user and an application. Rules are needed for transmissions between data bases. Anyone who has attempted to read a magnetic tape—when he or she was unsure of the tape format, parity, or number of tracks—can appreciate the problem of trying to communicate without knowing the rules.

Knowledge of the rules, however, is not enough to ensure effective communication; the rules must also be formalized. Rules that are formalized can be copied and supplied to all parties concerned, and they can be enforced in a uniform manner. They can be approved officially and adopted by an entire project. They can also be changed officially, because they will include a standard procedure for communicating the date and nature of the change to the entire project team. The difference between unformalized rules and formalized ones is the difference between trial-and-error work on the one hand and production level work on the other hand.

When the rules of data communications are formalized they are called protocols. The software objectives of the preceding chapter have led to the development of hundreds of data communications protocols. Protocols differ from network to network, application to application, manufacturer to manufacturer, and—with the larger manufacturers—from device type to device type within a product line.

Groups of Protocols For the purposes of discussion and standardization, we group these protocols into classes by level or layer. The word *level* initially distinguished hardware-oriented rules, or *low-level* considerations, from software-oriented rules, which have traditionally been called *higher level*. But the word *layer* is now also becoming popular. It reflects the fact that some protocols subsume, or are built upon, other protocols.

Either term accurately describes the relationships among the first three levels to be discussed here. The other levels differ from one another not so much by level of abstraction as by direction of emphasis. In other words, the protocols for users, data bases, and applications are part of a hierarchy which is concerned with the payload side of communications. Network-oriented protocols are part of the control side of communications. In the absence of a new term that is suitably descriptive, I have chosen to retain the term *level*.

This discussion of vocabulary is important because it helps establish the logical organization of protocols. In this book, we use the six levels of protocol used in ARPAnet literature and generally recognized within the industry, but other classifications do exist. Another data communications professional has explained the division of protocols into levels in the following way:

"Standards-making organizations . . . have divided protocols into layered architectures. Each distinct level clearly defines various data communications functions and logical operations. Each level is functionally independent of the others, but builds on those preceding it. To function, higher levels depend on correct operation of the lower levels. Data are transparent from higher to lower levels" (Weissberger, 1979).

The rest of this chapter describes the following six levels of protocol:

- Level 1—The hardware interface
- Level 2—The data link control
- Level 3—The message control
- Level 4—The applications control
- Level 5—The network control
- Level 6—Everything else

Figure 4-1 shows the relationship between these levels and the communications objectives of Chapter 3.

Level 1—The Hardware Interface

As we discussed in Chapter 2, the hardware interface is a physical entity used to connect a piece of digital equipment to the communications facility. The level 1 rules describe the significance of the signal on each of the circuits in the interface.

	Device	User	Data	Applica-tions	Net-work
1. Hardware interface	X				
2. Data link control	X				
3. Message control		X	X		
4. Applications control			X	X	
5. Network control					X
6. Other			X	X	

FIGURE 4-1. Communications Objectives Addressed by the Levels of Protocol

Level 2—Data Link Control

The level 2 rules are used by the software controlling a device; they distinguish·data from noise and they identify and correct errors.

Level 3—Message Control

The rules of message control show which messages are contained in the data of level 2 communications; they detect and correct errors involved in assembling these messages; and they indicate the destination of the messages.

Level 4—Applications Control

Level 4 rules vary from application to application within the same network and even within the same computer. They control the sequence of events between the computer's application and the user or another application. They also control the sequence of activities within the application itself.

Level 4 includes such diverse protocols as the following:

- The commands of an online text editor
- The logon/logoff sequences for a timesharing monitor
- The remote job entry commands for a computer utility
- The user's conversation with an interactive compiler
- The user input and output for a running computational program
- The query language of an information-retrieval application
- The procedures for an online inventory control system, a theater reservations system, or an airline reservations system

Level 5—Network Control

Network computers use the level 5 rules to inform one another of their status, of their priorities, and of their immediate or anticipated requirements. Level 5 rules supply the commands that processors with pivotal responsibilities in a network issue to their subordinates. These rules provide the mechanism by which the pivotal processors learn whether or not their commands have been obeyed.

Level 6—Everything Else

Level 6 includes various sets of rules. For example, it includes rules that expand the facilities of a single computer to encompass programs running on other computers within the network. It includes rules for copying or accessing remote files through local or remote data base management systems. Here also are the protocols by which programs on different computers can be executed synchronously so that they can work together on complex problems. Most of the advanced work in protocol development involves the protocols of level 6.

SUMMARY

We have seen that rules are necessary in order for devices to communicate. The rules are called protocols. Protocols are divided into levels. For discussion purposes, we will use six levels of protocol. The reader will encounter other systems with other levels of protocol, but the transition from the levels described in this book to the new levels should be obvious.

REFERENCES

Protocols

Davies, D. W.; Barber, D. L. A.; Price, W. L.; and Solomonides, C. M. *Computer Networks and Their Protocols.* New York: John Wiley and Sons, 1979.

Folts, H. C., and Karp, H. R. *McGraw-Hill's Compilation of Data Communications Standards.* New York: McGraw-Hill, 1978.

IBM. *Synchronous Data Link Control General Information Manual.* IBM Corp., GA 27-3093.

Microdata Corporation. "The Communications Handbook." Irvine, Calif.: Microdata Corp.

Standard Protocol Classifications

Weissberger, Alan J. "Orient Your Data-Link Protocols Toward Bits, Though Characters Still Count (Data Communications: Part Four)." *Electronic Design*, 19 July 1979, 15: 86–92.

ANSI X353's five levels are:
1. Hardware interface
2. DLC
3. Network control
4. System control
5. User control

ANSI DISY's six levels are:

1. Hardware interface
2. DLC
3. Transport control (message control)
4. Session control (dialogue control)
5. Presentation control
6. Process control

ISO's seven levels are:

1. Hardware interface
2. DLC
3. Network control
4. Transport control
5. Session control
6. Presentation control
7. Application control

5

Hardware Protocols—Their Functional Interpretation

This chapter takes a practical look at level 1 protocol, the rules that comprise the hardware interface. After a general description of the hardware interface, we explain the functions of one of the most common interfaces, the RS-232C, and give an example of this interface "in action." To balance the picture, we then look at some of the limitations of the RS-232C, and we introduce some of the topics to be covered in Chapter 6 by describing the relationship between the hardware interface and data link control.

The Hardware Interface

Its Purpose   The hardware protocols that are specified in the manufacturing standards of the electronics industry allow a terminal made by one company to be connected to a computer made by another company. These same rules also make it possible for two dissimilar computers or two dissimilar terminals to communicate with each other.

There is an analogous situation in software, where the calling sequence of one module is compatible with the receiving sequence of another module. This allows two modules to be linked and executed together successfully. For both hardware and software, the protocol goes by the same name: it is called an interface.

The Plug-and-Socket Interface A common form of hardware interface is a pair of male and female connectors, as shown in Figure 5-1. Each pin of the male plug and its corresponding hole in the female socket have a particular meaning that is specified by the protocol, or *standard*. Of course, the actual hardware implementation of a standard interface need not be a plug. It is enough that each *circuit*, represented in Figure 5-1 by a pin/hole pair, be clearly defined both as to its function and the electrical signal that it carries. Then, regardless of the mechanism used to terminate that circuit on one side of the interface, an engineer can make the connection with the corresponding circuit of the other machine, using a compatible mechanism. Examples include wire-to-wire and optical-sender/optical-receiver mechanisms.

A plug and socket combination, however, is a convenient way to package a hardware interface implementing a particular

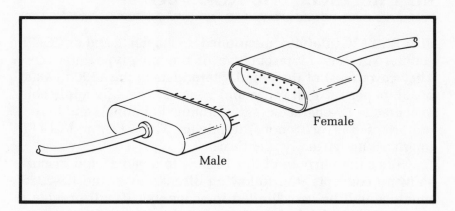

Female

Male

FIGURE 5-1. Male and Female Plugs of the Hardware Interface

specification. It is even more convenient if the specification of that interface contains not only the minimum circuits that will be used for a given combination of computer and terminal but also some additional functions that are relevant to other terminals and computers in the same class. (By *class* we mean those computers and terminals that are used in similar applications and that operate in compatible speed ranges and under similar conditions.)

The Work of Standards Organizations   The national and international standards organizations are responsible for the development of hardware interfaces for various classes of computers or terminals. For our purposes we will restrict our discussion to the interfaces developed by the national organization, the Electronics Industries Association (EIA), and its international counterpart, the International Consultative Committee for Telegraphy and Telephony (CCITT). The latter organization is a division of the International Telecommunications Union. For additional information on these two groups and on the interfaces for which they have published standards, the reader should refer directly to the organization, to the McGraw-Hill *Data Communications Standards*, or to the books listed in the References section under "Hardware Interfaces."

Example of an Interface: The RS-232C

EIA's RS-232C interface, mentioned in Chapter 2, and its CCITT counterparts are representative of the plug-type interfaces. They cover most of the popular terminals in the 1200 to 4800 bps (bits per second) range and hence are equally applicable to character-by-character (asynchronous) terminals and to record-oriented (synchronous) terminals. These EIA and CCITT interfaces are virtually identical.

Since the purpose of this book is to organize and discuss software concepts, the following discussion of the RS-232C interface will be very limited in scope, but it will provide a specific point of reference for understanding as much as we need of the hardware interface.

Standard Configurations Some terminals and computers, notably terminals used with minicomputers, are connected directly to each other through an RS-232C interface, as shown in Figure 5-2. However, most hookups involve a communications line (*analog*) and modems for converting digital signals from the terminals and computers and analog signals from the communications medium (see Figure 5-3). Most RS-232Cs are used with modems, and that is the configuration we will use here.

Interface A in Figure 5-3 is unaware of interface B. Interface A is also unaware of any devices beyond the modem. Fig-

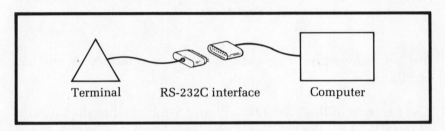

FIGURE 5-2. Direct Terminal-to-Computer Hookup Using RS-232C Plug

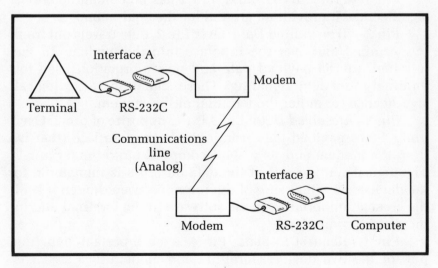

FIGURE 5-3. Terminal-to-Computer Hookup via Modems Using RS-232C Plugs

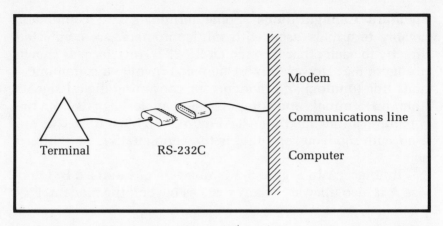

FIGURE 5-4. Terminal-to-Computer Hookup Viewed from the Terminal Using the RS-232C Interface

ure 5-4 shows how this system looks to interface A and its terminal.

The Circuits of the RS-232C   Figure 5-5 identifies the circuits of the RS-232C. We shall describe their functions briefly, identifying, where possible, the software implications of each circuit.

Pin 1—Protective Ground: Pin 1 has no communications significance. It provides a ground for the equipment.

Pin 2—Transmitted Data: Over Pin 2, data travels out from the terminal and over the interface into the modem. To the terminal, this is payload data and not information used for terminal-to-modem signaling. These signals have no logical significance for either the terminal or the modem.

Pin 3—Received Data: Pin 3 is the opposite of pin 2. Over pin 3 flows payload data from outside the interface (that is, from the modem and its distant computer) into the terminal. The logical significance of the data on pin 3 is immaterial to the devices on either side of the interface, even though it is of the greatest importance to the software in the terminal and in the distant computer.

Pin 4—Request to Send: Pin 4 is an important signaling pin for the two devices, terminal and modem. If a signal is present on this circuit, it means that the terminal is requesting permission to send data over pin 2. There is no possible ambiguity because the signal on this pin can only be set by the terminal and it can have only one interpretation according to the rules.

Pin 5—Clear to Send: Pin 5 is the complementary circuit to pin 4. Pin 5 is turned on by the modem when the modem is prepared to accept data over the interface through pin 2.

Pin 6—Data Set Ready: Pin 6 is a status circuit. The modem keeps this pin "on" to indicate that the modem is fully operational.

Pin 7—Signal Ground: Pin 7 is the common ground used by all signals; it has no communications significance.

Pin 8—Received Line Signal Detector: The modem uses pin 8 to inform the terminal that a carrier of sufficient strength is present. In some dial-up systems, software interprets the presence of a signal on this circuit as an indication that a call has come in. This is not a standard interpretation. In fact, no standard interpretation has successfully been enforced for this pin. Some systems, for example, deduce an incoming call from the presence of a signal on pin 22.

Pin 9 and Pin 10: Pins 9 and 10 are used for hardware testing. They have no significance to software in the terminal.

Pin 11: No function is assigned to this pin in the standard.

Pin 12—Secondary Received Line Signal Detector: Pin 12 is analogous to pin 8; both tell the terminal that a channel is available. Pin 8 refers to the channel that carries signals for pins 2 and 3, or the *primary channel.* Pin 12 refers to the channel that handles signals for pins 14 and 16. This channel may be called the *secondary channel.*

Pin 13—Secondary Clear to Send: Pin 13 is analogous to pin 5. Pin 5 indicates the modem's readiness to receive a transmission over the primary channel; pin 13 indicates the same thing for the secondary channel.

Pin 14—Secondary Transmitted Data: Pin 14 sends payload data from the terminal over the interface using the secondary channel.

Pin 15—Transmit Timing: The modem uses pin 15 to transmit timing if the modem supplies the clocking for the bits transmitted over pin 2. This process is referred to as *external clocking.*

Pin No.	Circuit Designation	CCITT Equiv.	Direction	Description
1	AA	101	Both	Protective Ground
2	BA	103	To modem	Transmitted Data
3	BB	104	To terminal	Received Data
4	CA	105	To modem	Request to Send
5	CB	106	To terminal	Clear to Send
6	CC	107	To terminal	Data Set Ready
7	AB	102	Both	Signal Ground (Common Return)
8	CF	109	To terminal	Received Line Signal Detector
9	–	–	–	(Reserved for modem testing)
10	–	–	–	(Reserved for modem testing)
11				Unassigned
12	SCF	122	To terminal	Secondary Received Line Signal Detector

Pin No.	Circuit Designation	CCITT Equiv.	Direction	Description
13	SCB	121	To terminal	Secondary Clear to Send
14	SBA	118	To modem	Secondary Transmitted Data
15	DB	114	To terminal	Transmit Timing (DCE Source)
16	SBB	119	To terminal	Secondary Received Data
17	DD	115	To terminal	Receive Timing (DCE Source)
18				Unassigned
19	SCA	120	To modem	Secondary Request to Send
20	CD	108.2	To modem	Data Terminal Ready
21	CG	110	Either	Signal Quality Detector
22	CE	125	To terminal	Ring Indicator
23	CH/CI	111	Either	Data Rate Selector (DTE/DCE)
24	DA	113	To modem	Transmit Timing (DTE Source)
25				Unassigned

FIGURE 5-5. RS-232C Interface Circuits

Pin 16—Secondary Received Data: Pin 16 is used by the terminal for receiving payload data from the interface using the secondary channel.

Pin 17—Receive Timing: Pin 17 is used by the modem if the modem supplies the clocking for bits received over pin 3.

Pin 18: Pin 18, like pin 11, is unassigned.

Pin 19—Secondary Request to Send: Pin 19 is analogous to pin 4. Pin 19 represents a request from the terminal for permission to send data over pin 14 using the secondary channel.

Pin 20—Data Terminal Ready: Pin 20 is the complement to pin 6. Pin 20 is kept in the "on" position by the terminal to indicate that the terminal is functional.

Pin 21—Signal Quality Detector: Pin 21 may be set or reset by either device to indicate that device's evaluation of the signal quality received over the communications line. The terminal perceives signal quality through analysis of the data pulses on pins 2, 3, 14, and 16. The modem uses the actual analog medium to which the modem is attached.

Pin 22—Ring Indicator: Pin 22 represents a circuit that is turned on by the modem when it detects a ringing signal on the communications line.

Pin 23—Data Rate Selector: Pin 23 is set or reset by either device to indicate which of two speeds for data transmission should be provided; in other words, it indicates what clock rate should be used.

Pin 24—Transmit Timing: Pin 24 is exactly the same as pin 15 except that the timing pulse originates with the terminal and is referred to as *internal clocking.*

Pin 25: Pin 25, like pins 11 and 18, is unassigned.

Example of the Interface in Use

The twenty-five pins described above represent a set of twenty-five binary switches—eighteen if we omit grounds, unassigned pins, and modem-testing pins. Having eighteen binary switches means that the devices can indicate 2^{18} or 262,144 possible logical conditions. We will see, however, that there are only about a dozen valid states in which the two devices can communicate meaningfully, so we deduce that, by identifying the right combinations of on/off conditions in the eighteen pins and by resetting these pins as required, we can achieve sufficient dialogue between the two devices for the needs of data communications. The following example, described first without pins and then with pins, shows that our deduction is correct.

An Outline of the Communication Process   Let us say that the terminal has a message to send to the computer. The terminal must first notify the modem that it needs to use the data channel. The modem must answer and indicate that the line is clear. The terminal will then send its data, utilizing the registers and bit timing of its controllers. After the transmission has been completed, the terminal will check for any detectable errors.

Communication Using the Interface Circuits   The indicated scenario can be achieved through careful use of the various circuits of the interface. First, the terminal notifies the modem of its need to transmit by turning on pin 4, Request to Send. Next, the modem turns on pin 5, Clear to Send, which means "go ahead." The terminal's controller places the bits of data to be transmitted on pin 2 (Transmitted Data) in serial fashion, that is one by one, with matching clock pulses on pin 24 (Transmit Timing).

To the extent that it can perform any error detection at this time, the terminal will check the setting of pins 8, Received Line Signal Detector, and 21, Signal Quality Detector, after data transmission is completed. To do any further error checking would require a dialogue with the receiving computer. (This kind of dialogue, of course, requires one of the higher levels of protocol.) However, it is obvious that just the half dozen pins that were used in this example were adequate for the fundamental forms of data transmission.

Limitations of the RS-232C

An example like the above might lead to the conclusion that the RS-232C interface and its equivalents would be sufficient for communication needs for years to come. Unfortunately this is not the case. The RS-232C standard is not adequate for future needs.

First of all, the RS-232C logic provides only two choices of timing speed. Many terminals now available can operate in at least four different speeds—10 cps (characters per second), 15 cps, 30 cps, and 300 cps—all available in the same device and manually selectable with a rotary switch. The RS-232C is limited to two of these speed options.

Then there is the two-sided problem of the interpretation of the standard and the enforcement of the standard. As we mentioned earlier, some facilities use pin 8 and some use pin 22 to initiate two-way communication in a dial-up system. Which interpretation is the correct one and why have users not been consistent? Furthermore, pins 11, 18, and 25 are officially unassigned, yet they are used and the uses vary from installation to installation.

Finally, although some systems do permit the data communications software to select the particular channel (primary or secondary) to be used for a particular transmission, usually the primary/secondary channel hookup is not under software control. This means that there is no standard for the use of secondary channel pins (pins 12, 13, 14, 16, and 19), and thus the RS-232C two-channel capability cannot be used consistently. (For further discussion of the use of primary and secondary channels, see the References section.)

These few comments about the interface point out some of the limitations. Currently, new standards for hardware interfaces are being developed by the various standards groups, and in the next few years we will see several of them in established use. The new standards will permit more flexible and efficient network control as well as make direct use of hardware features built into newer terminals.

The Relationship to Data Link Control

Before we leave the protocol level of the hardware interface, we must consider how this level looks to the software. The hardware interface is the first level of protocol; the next level of protocol is data link control. In this section, we will examine the relationship between the two levels of protocol. In other words, the concept of protocol as an interface means that it encompasses not only the interface between entities (devices or modules, for example) at the same level, but also the interface between different levels. Figure 5-6 illustrates these relationships.

The Functions of the Controller   The data link control software does not deal directly with the interface. Instead, the software deals with an interpretation of the interface provided to it by the controller. This interpretation is contained in the digital registers of the controller, which are manipulated by the software. Figure 5-7 sketches the controller's logical position between the terminal or computer and the hardware interface.

An ideal data link control program would know exactly what was happening on the interface. Specifically, the software is interested in knowing:

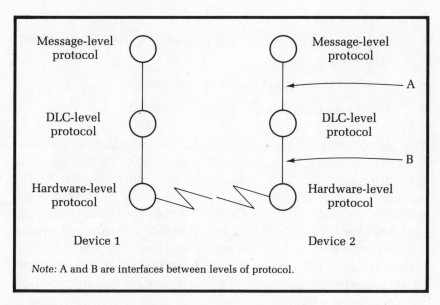

Note: A and B are interfaces between levels of protocol.

FIGURE 5-6.   Interfaces between Levels of Protocol

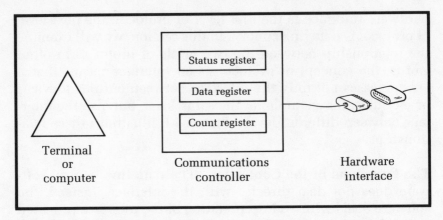

FIGURE 5-7. Controller's Position between the Terminal or Computer and the Hardware Interface

- Whether its data have been transmitted (on both primary and secondary channels)

- Whether the incoming data have been received (on both channels)

- Whether it is all right to send data (on both channels)

- Whether the modem is functional

- Whether there is a carrier present on the line (for both channels)

- Whether the signal quality is adequate

- Whether a ring signal has been detected

The above, including information for the two channels, makes a total of eleven different binary conditions. The software is also interested in the condition of the controller itself—for example, the results of parity analysis on incoming data, whether the controller was able to finish its communication, and whether the controller is functional at the time of inquiry. These conditions, while not an exhaustive list, total fourteen binary states, all of which are vitally important to the software. In my experience, no controller provides all of this information directly to the software.

Instead, the controller typically combines information about these conditions (using OR and AND operations) into an eight-bit register, (or it combines them with count information into a sixteen-bit register). The software may interrogate this status register through a program-controlled data transfer that treats the controller as a local device (which it is). *Program-controlled data transfer* uses a command such as READ DIRECT to transfer the contents of the controller's status register into one of the CPU's general purpose registers. The software then deduces the desired information through a series of masking operations that allow individual bits or combinations of bits to be tested.

The problem with such an arrangement is that the software can only get a general impression of the "goodness" or "badness" of a transmission. The information that it gets is not sufficiently detailed for effective error analysis. It may be argued that detailed error analysis is the province of hardware monitors; this position is reasonable enough for development work but not for an operational network.

The Programmer's Role   Not all controllers operate in the same way. They vary from "smart" controllers, which do a great deal of the work for the software, to very rudimentary controllers. Regardless of the sophistication of the controller, however, the software programmer must realize that, whatever the effect he or she wishes to achieve in a distant terminal, it can only be accomplished by writing code that affects three separate devices—the CPU on which the code executes, the controller (whose registers the code manipulates and which is the programmer's only contact with the interface), and the terminal where the desired objective is to be achieved.

To write effective code, the programmer must be intimately familiar with the operation of each of the three devices. Operational information on computers is comparatively easy to obtain. Computer CPU manuals are usually well written and are designed for the programmer to use. The same can generally be said of information about terminals. Controllers, on the other hand, have traditionally been poorly documented. This is probably because controllers come from specialized shops; they are built to connect the computers from one manufacturer with the terminals from another manufacturer or to connect a product line of terminals with a product line of CPU's from the same manufacturer. In other words, they are a product of engineers who are working to meet the requirements of other engineers, not of programmers. In any event, the programmer must study the controller manuals carefully and translate them into software terms and procedures.

While the programmer does not deal directly with the interface, it is a good idea to obtain the specifications for it nonetheless. The interface imposes a physical limit on what can be accomplished over the communications line, and its specifications will show these operational characteristics. For example, the interface's operational characteristics establish an upper bound on the transmission rate for the communications line (of course, the controller and the terminal, as well as the modem, also set upper bounds—the resulting transmission speed is going to be the smallest of the four).

SUMMARY

What we have learned about interfaces in this chapter may be summarized as follows: the interface is accessible to software only through the intermediation of the communications controller. The interface permits machine-to-machine recognition of request and go-ahead conditions, detects incoming rings, provides a clocking circuit so that bits may be properly interpreted, and provides circuits for monitoring line status. That is all. Any other desired functions, such as making a terminal perform basic mechanical actions (line feed or erase, for example), must be encoded into data and transmitted over the data circuits of the interface. Then, when those functions have been received as data at the terminal, they may be decoded and acted upon.

Even though some software functions, such as parity checking and forward error correction, are performed by smart controllers, the error codes used look like data to the interface and are thus transparent to the level 1 hardware protocol. In other words, all of the really interesting (to programmers) network and terminal operations are communicated at the software levels of protocol. Chapter 6 introduces the discussion of these software protocols.

REFERENCES

Hardware Interfaces

International Telegraph and Telephone Consultative Committee. *Data Transmission Over the Telephone Network.* Recommendation v. 24. Sixth Plenary Assembly, International Telecommunication Union, vol. VIII.1, Geneva, 1977.

Primary and Secondary Channels

The following discussion indicates the variety of ways in which primary and secondary channels are currently used:

(1) A *half-duplex channel used in full-duplex mode* operates on a two-wire communications line; this is often referred to as reverse-channel operation. Usually, the secondary channel occupies a smaller proportion of the bandwidth of the communications line than does the primary channel. The primary channel is used for communication in one direction and the secondary channel for communication in the opposite direction. The aggregate bandwidth of the primary and secondary channel is less than the total capacity of the line because there must be a separation band between the two channels. Either channel or both may be reversed with the usual modem delay for line turnaround.

(2) A *half-duplex channel used in half-duplex mode* operates on a two-wire communications line. Only the primary channel is used. The bandwidth is equal to the line's capacity. Turnaround requires the usual modem delay.

(3) A *full-duplex channel used in full-duplex mode* operates on a four-wire communications line. To distinguish this mode from the reverse-channel type of operation, I often use the term "full full-duplex." It is not an elegant term, but it is unambiguous. This mode uses both the primary and secondary channels. If transmission is always on one channel and reception always on the other, all line turnaround problems are eliminated. Since there is the equivalent of a dedicated communications line for each channel, the aggregate bandwidth is twice that of the communications line.

(4) A *full-duplex channel used in half-duplex mode* is a software limitation imposed upon a full full-duplex operation. Here the software requires the hardware to act as if only a half-duplex facility

were available. The software, not the hardware, accepts transmission in only one direction at a time, although both channels are connected. No line turnaround delay is ever encountered so this mode is certainly more efficient than half-duplex channels used in half-duplex mode, but it does not realize the full potential of the full duplex channel.

User-Oriented Communications

Gruenberger, Fred, ed. *The Transition to On-Line Computing.* Washington, D. C.: Thomson Book Co., 1967.

Orr, William D., ed. *Conversational Computers.* New York: John Wiley and Sons, 1968.

6

Software Protocols—Their Functional Composition

This chapter provides a brief discussion of the protocols of data communications software and the influence of structured programming on their functional composition. We then build the framework for the material in the next two chapters by grouping the software functions according to the type of work they perform.

Relationships Among Protocols, Functions, and Modules

The objective of software is to make something happen inside a computer. With data communications it is fairly easy to come up with a list of things that need to happen. The difficulty comes in trying to impose some organization upon those tasks so that a system may be developed.

61

Let us call these tasks the *functions* of data communications. How should these functions be organized? Software, after all, is executable code, and code is organized in three ways—geographically, temporally, and administratively.

Definitions *Geographic* organization deals with the spatial relationships of code within memory. Code is compiled or assembled in *modules*. Modules in turn are loaded into adjacent or prespecified parts of memory.

Temporal organization deals with the sequence in which code executes. In a conventional CPU, code is executed one instruction after another. The sequence may be (a) prescribed and unvarying or (b) disjointed. In a disjointed sequence, segments of code are still executed in a prescribed and unvarying way, but the order of the individual segments is variable.

Administrative organization deals with the control that one set of code has over another and the responsibility that one set has for satisfying the requirements of the other. In conventionally organized code, a main program "controls" the subroutine that it calls. The subroutine is "responsible" for supplying a certain result to the main program.

Recent developments in structured programming indicate that code is more reliable when geographic organization reflects administrative organization—in other words, when modules are located in a hierarchy based on responsibility. Temporal organization has produced only a few guidelines, namely that (a) the fewer segments the more efficient is the code and (b) the more predictable a sequence is, the more easily validated the software of which it forms a part.

The Influence of Structured Programming Structured programming techniques dictate that the functions of data communications will be organized into modules administratively—according to their control and responsibility. Figure 6-1 shows the hierarchical structure of these relationships, which we developed in Chapter 4. Figure 6-2 gives the more detailed structure of the software that develops as the data communications functions are separated into some modules and distributed over others; the chapters that follow will describe these modules. Each large box in Figure 6-2 represents a mod-

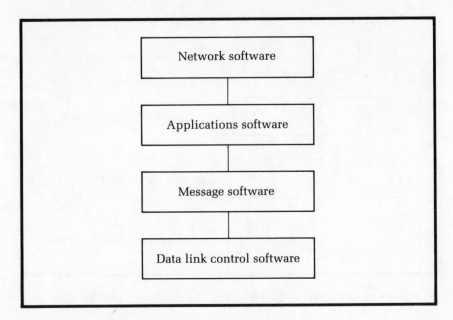

FIGURE 6-1. Hierarchy of Communications Software

ule. The smaller boxes are submodules. The most reliable software results from limiting each submodule to one function.

The first task, before writing the code for the data communications functions, is the identification and analysis of those functions. We have organized the functions by *type* in order to make them more understandable. This organization by type has very little to do with the actual sequence in which the functions are written or the sequence in which they are executed in the computer. It is simply a convenient means of organizing the functions for the purpose of discussion. These functions fall into two general categories: the hardware-supporting functions and the software-supporting functions.

Hardware-Supporting Functions

(1) *Line functions*: These functions are directly involved with the communications controller and, through it, with the communications line.

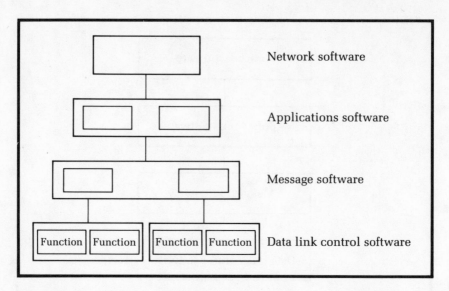

FIGURE 6-2. Modules in the Hierarchy of Communications Service

(2) *Device functions:* These functions perform the device-specific operations that vary according to the different characteristics of the devices in the network.

(3) *Presentation functions:* These make transformations on data according to the external, or user-oriented, requirements.

Software-Supporting Functions

(1) *Executive functions:* These control the sequence in which tasks are accomplished; they occasionally initiate and supervise the actions as well.

(2) *Directive functions:* These functions make decisions about what commitments of resources should be made and in what quantities. Executive functions carry out the decisions of directive functions.

(3) *Quality-assurance functions:* These functions operate as safeguards for the data communications system. They monitor what is happening and provide whatever is needed in the way of fallback capability.

(4) *Intersystem functions:* These functions act as interfaces between the other data communications functions and the host computer environment.

SUMMARY

This chapter has shown that software protocols are implemented through a set of functions. Functions are organized into modules for execution on the computer. The most reliable systems result from imposing a hierarchical relationship upon the modules and limiting the modules so that each submodule consists of one function.

The functions are then classified by type in preparation for the next chapters.

REFERENCES

Principles of Structured Programming

Glass, Robert L. *Software Reliability Guidebook* Englewood Cliffs, N. J.: Prentice-Hall, Inc., 1979.

McGowan, Clement L., and Kelly, John R. *Top-Down Structured Programming Techniques.* New York: Petrocelli/Charter, 1975.

Myers, Glenford J. *The Art of Software Testing.* New York: John Wiley and Sons, 1979.

Myers, Glenford J. *Composite/Structured Design.* New York: Van Nostrand Reinhold Co., 1978.

Myers, Glenford J. *Reliable Software through Composite Design.* New York: Petrocelli/Charter, 1975.

Yourdon, Edward. *Techniques of Program Structure and Design.* Englewood Cliffs, N.J.: Prentice-Hall, Inc., 1975.

7

The Hardware-
Supporting
Functions

*In this chapter we discuss the hardware-supporting functions
introduced in Chapter 6: line functions, device functions, and
presentation functions.*

Line Functions

The line functions include data link control and interrupt handling.

Data Link Control   *Data link control* is the software function
that interacts directly with the communications controller and
the line adapter hardware. All communications data going out
of or coming into the computer pass through data link control.
Chapter 2 explained the way that data link control works. A
communications package that has both asynchronous and synchronous traffic usually has a different data link control for

each. Similarly, if the controller presents the input channel and the output channel as separate lines, the system will probably have two data link controls—one for input and one for output.

Interrupt Handling *Interrupt handling* is a very specialized line function. It allows the state of the machine to be changed from one software process to another and back again, as illustrated in Figure 7-1. For instance, let us say that the computer is in the midst of carrying out a long computational sequence when a data transmission arrives at the controller. A status line is activated by the controller. If the status line has high enough priority to break into the operation in process, then the computational sequence in the CPU is "interrupted." The current memory address is saved, and the computer begins executing at a predefined place in memory, which is the first address of the interrupt handling routine. Sometimes the predefined

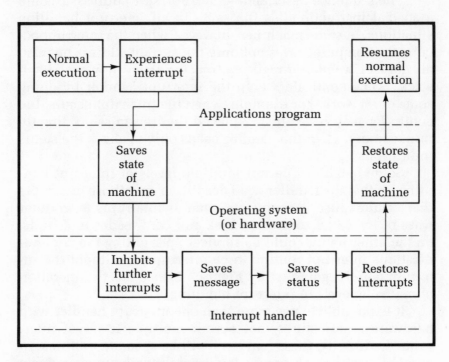

FIGURE 7-1. Interrupt Handling

place is only one instruction long. In that case, the instruction contains a transfer to the actual starting location of the interrupt routine. The result is the same.

The objectives of the interrupt handling routine are to get the incoming message into a safe place before something happens to it and to preserve any volatile status information from the controller pertinent to that message. After satisfying these objectives, the interrupt handler must get out of the way as soon as possible. There are two reasons for this. First, the computational activity must be resumed so that the computer can get on with its other work. Second, when an interrupt handler is operating, it normally turns off (inhibits) other interrupts in order to avoid being interrupted itself. This means the interrupt handler runs the risk of losing other transmissions while the handler is doing its job so it is best to finish that job as soon as possible. Some controllers can queue up interrupts, but there is a limit to how many can be in queue waiting for the interrupt handler.

The sequence described—interrupt, save address, execute a special instruction—is the same in all interrupt handling situations. In some machines, however, when the interrupt occurs, the computer saves not only the current address but also all the CPU's volatile registers, placing them in a pushdown stack. Some controllers help the interrupt handler by doing some of its work. For example, when the interrupt occurs, the controller may have already placed the transmission directly into memory. Then the handler needs only to check the status indications.

Some machines permit multiple levels of interrupt handling, so that the handler need deactivate only those interrupts that would cause it confusion, such as interrupts from other lines of the same controller. Disk and card-reader interrupts, on the other hand, could be serviced, permitting the communications interrupt routine to be interrupted, without the interrupt handler going astray. Figure 7-2 diagrams the operation of multiple levels of interrupt handling.

It is possible to use more than one interrupt handler with hardware architectures that permit multiple levels of interrupts. Ordinarily, these handlers will be separate routines; in a machine with stack-processing capabilities, however, a single reentrant routine can do the job. The stack automatically pro-

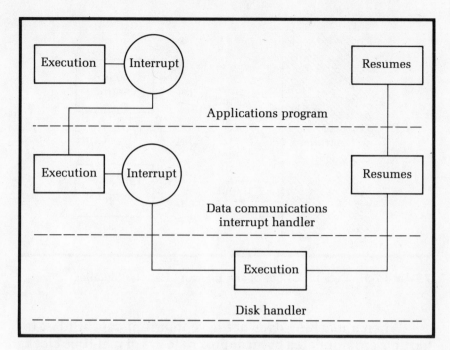

FIGURE 7-2. Multiple Levels of Interrupt Handling

vides temporary storage for working registers when a higher priority interrupt causes momentary suspension of lower priority work.

An interrupt handler for data communications can be viewed as a subroutine of the data link control module (see Figure 7-3); the call from data link control is not in real time but the return is in real time. Note that the interrupt handler operates in real time where the data link control routine need not do so. The economics of computers, specifically, the demands of resource management, require an absolute minimum of real-time work. This is another reason why the time spent in the interrupt handler must be as brief as possible. This usually means keeping the number of its executable instructions as small as possible. Moreover, since interrupt handling is a machine-oriented function that ought to be transparent to calling modules, it must also be as reliable as possible. Both these considerations imply that interrupt handling should be as simple as possible and should contain a minimum number of instructions.

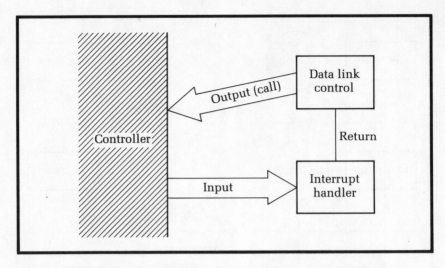

FIGURE 7-3. Data Link Control and Interrupt Handler Modules

When a machine does not have interrupt capabilities, interrupts are simulated by an appropriate use of real-time clocks or by having a software scheduler that continually monitors the data communications line.

Device Functions

The device functions include code conversion, blocking and deblocking, buffering, device handling, and device management.

Code Conversion *Code conversion* is the function of translating from the character-oriented code sequence of one computer into the code sequence of another—for example, from ASCII into EBCDIC. The principle involved is a simple one-for-one substitution. As with many other things in data communications, the principle may be straightforward, but the implementation is not.

One implementational difficulty lies in the mechanics of making the translation. Table lookup is the only feasible way. Let us use ASCII and EBCDIC as examples (see Figures 7-4 and 7-5, respectively). The reader should note, first of all, that ASCII

b_7						0 0 0	0 0 1	0 1 0	0 1 1	1 0 0	1 0 1	1 1 0	1 1 1
Bits	b_4	b_3	b_2	b_1	Column → / Row ↓	0	1	2	3	4	5	6	7
	0	0	0	0	0	NUL	DLE	SP	0	@	P	`	p
	0	0	0	1	1	SOH	DC1	!	1	A	Q	a	q
	0	0	1	0	2	STX	DC2	"	2	B	R	b	r
	0	0	1	1	3	ETX	DC3	#	3	C	S	c	s
	0	1	0	0	4	EOT	DC4	$	4	D	T	d	t
	0	1	0	1	5	ENQ	NAK	%	5	E	U	e	u
	0	1	1	0	6	ACK	SYN	&	6	F	V	f	v
	0	1	1	1	7	BEL	ETB	'	7	G	W	g	w
	1	0	0	0	8	BS	CAN	(	8	H	X	h	x
	1	0	0	1	9	HT	EM	)	9	I	Y	i	y
	1	0	1	0	10	LF	SUB	*	:	J	Z	j	z
	1	0	1	1	11	VT	ESC	+	;	K	[	k	{
	1	1	0	0	12	FF	FS	,	<	L	/	l	|
	1	1	0	1	13	CR	GS	−	=	M	]	m	}
	1	1	1	0	14	SO	RS	.	>	N	^	n	~
	1	1	1	1	15	SI	US	/	?	O	_	o	DEL

FIGURE 7-4. American National Standard Code for Information Interchange

bits are numbered from right to left and EBCDIC bits are numbered in the opposite direction. Obviously, any formula that might be suggested for performing an algorithmic translation (adding leading bits, reversing certain bits, and so on) cannot be consistently applied. The most efficient technique for conversion is table lookup. Table lookup requires only a single instruction to find the new value—a register-load instruction with an offset equal to the value of the old character.

There are two problems with ASCII-to-EBCDIC table lookup in this example. Both problems require resolution early in the development cycle for every new data communications system. First, the two tables are of unequal length. ASCII can readily be mapped into EBCDIC since there are only 128 ASCII characters to 256 of EBCDIC. What about going the other way? Some provision, such as a dummy pattern, must be made to preserve the one-instruction translation economy. Code con-

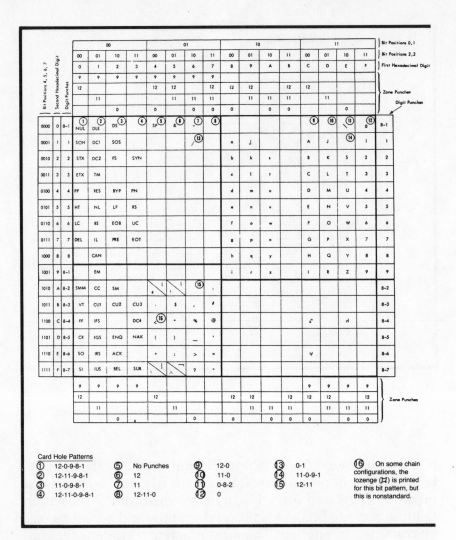

FIGURE 7-5. Extended Binary Coded Decimal Interchange Code

version should never involve error checking; that is too expensive a feature for such an elementary operation.

The second problem is that for some characters there are no direct equivalents. This is a definitional problem and is independent of the length of the code sets. There are some characters in one code set for which there are no characters with equivalent meanings in the other code set. This incompatibility occurs in the set of special characters (the *control*,

Control Character Representations

ACK	Acknowledge	EOT	End of Transmission	RES	Restore
BEL	Bell	ESC	Escape	RS	Reader Stop
BS	Backspace	ETB	End of Transmission Block	SI	Shift In
BYP	Bypass	ETC	End of Text	SM	Set Mode
CAN	Cancel	FF	Form Feed	SMM	Start of Manual Message
CC	Cursor Control	FS	Field Separator	SO	Shift Out
CR	Carriage Return	HT	Horizontal Tab	SOH	Start of Heading
CU1	Customer Use 1	IFS	Interchange File Separator	SOS	Start of Significance
CU2	Customer Use 2	IGS	Interchange Group Separator	SP	Space
CU3	Customer Use 3	IL	Idle	STX	Start of Text
DC1	Device Control 1	IRS	Interchange Record Separator	SUB	Substitute
DC2	Device Control 2	IUS	Interchange Unit Separator	SYN	Synchronous Idle
DC3	Device Control 3	LC	Lower Case	TM	Tape Mark
DC4	Device Control 4	LF	Line Feed	UC	Upper Case
DEL	Delete	NAK	Negative Acknowledge	VT	Vertical Tab
DLE	Data Link Escape	NL	New Line		
DS	Digit Select	NUL	Null		
EM	End of Medium	PF	Punch Off		
ENQ	Enquiry	PN	Punch On		

Special Graphic Characters

¢	Cent Sign	-	Minus Sign, Hyphen	∫	Hook
.	Period, Decimal Point	/	Slash	Ⴤ	Fork
<	Less-than Sign	,	Comma	⊣	Chair
(	Left Parenthesis	%	Percent		
+	Plus Sign	—	Underscore		
|	Logical OR, Absolute	>	Greater-than Sign		
&	Ampersand	?	Question Mark		
!	Exclamation Point	:	Colon		
$	Dollar Sign	#	Number Sign		
*	Asterisk	@	At Sign		
)	Right Parenthesis	'	Prime, Apostrophe		
;	Semicolon	=	Equal Sign		
¬	Logical NOT	"	Quotation Mark		
[	Left Bracket	\	Backslash		
]	Right Bracket	>	Circumflex		

or nongraphic, characters). Sometimes the special characters have equivalent significance but different names in the two code sets. Figure 7-6 shows the special characters and their various names, including, where possible, all the different names that are currently in use for the same character.

Other implementational difficulties lie in putting too many subfunctions into code conversion. Sometimes code conversion is done in conjunction with parity error checking, using table lookup to detect bad patterns. However, since the

EBCDIC (Hex) Pattern	ASCII	Common Name of Character	Other Name	Meaning
00	00	NUL		Null
01	01	SOH		Start of header
02	02	STX		Start of text
03	03	ETX		End of text
04	04	EOT		End of transmission
05	09	HT	PT	Horizontal tab (position)
06	06	ACK		Acknowledge (positive)
07	07	BEL		Bell
08	08	BS	EOM	Backspace, end of message
09	05	ENQ		Enquiry
0A	15	NAK		Acknowledge (negative)
0B	0B	VT		Vertical tab
0C	0C	FF		Form feed
0D	0D	CR		Carriage return
0E	0E	SO		Shift out
0F	0F	SI		Shift in
10	10	DLE		Data link escape

EBCDIC (Hex) Pattern	ASCII	Common Name of Character	Other Name	Meaning
11	11	DC1	SBA	Device control 1
12	12	DC2	EUA	Device control 2
13	13	DC3	IC	Device control 3
14	14	DC4	RA	Device control 4
15	0A	LF	NL	Line feed, next line
16	16	SYN		Synch
17	17	ETB		End of transmission block
18	18	CAN		Cancel
19	19	EM		End of medium
1A	1A	SS	SUB	Start of special sequence
1B	1B	ESC		Escape
1C	1C	FS	DUP	File separator
1D	1D	GS	SF	Group separator
1E	1E	RS	FM	Record separator
1F	1F	US	ITB	Unit separator, end intermediate transmission block
FF	FF	DEL		Delete

FIGURE 7-6. Special Characters

ASCII parity bit is not calculated in any standard way, the code conversion function must provide for all the possible situations found in different types of terminals:

- Parity bit set to even parity

- Parity bit set to odd parity

- Parity bit always set to zero

- Parity bit always set to one

- Parity bit ignored and generated randomly

This is an unnecessary complication.

Code conversion should be viewed as a service facility to higher level functions, as shown in Figure 7-7. However, data link control and code conversion can be combined without causing excessive overhead in an echoplexing system. The term *echoplexing* refers to an asynchronous environment where each character from the terminal is echoed back by the central processor. Actually, echoplexing is applied to synchronous transmissions as well, as a very high-overhead form of ARQ—or "advise repeat request"—error checking.

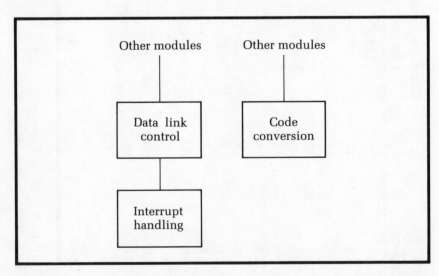

FIGURE 7-7. The Relationship of DLC, Interrupt, and Code Conversion Modules

Figure 7-8 shows the character A being transmitted from the terminal and being returned to the terminal by the CPU. Notice that the central processor contains input buffers for incoming characters, as well as output buffers for the outgoing characters. Note also that outgoing data consist of both echoed characters and characters that have originated in the CPU as part of the terminal-computer dialogue. Echoplexing, as this example illustrates, is often used in a terminal-oriented network where the user plays the role of an error-checking routine, verifying each character that is returned from the mainframe.

Blocking and Deblocking   *Blocking/deblocking* is the process of fitting a data transmission of given length into storage areas

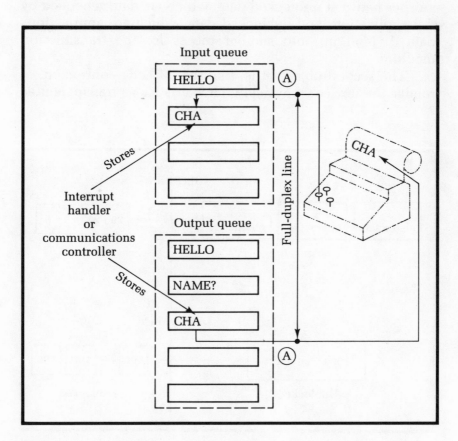

FIGURE 7-8.   Echoplexing Protocol

of other lengths and back again. The transformation is typically from a file-oriented or user-oriented record size into a device-oriented record size and vice versa.

This process is designed to meet two objectives. The first objective is to make the most efficient, and sometimes the only possible, use of a device. For example, a remote card reader might deal in transmissions of exactly 80 characters in length, requiring that records of more than 80 characters be broken up into 80-character chunks or that smaller ones be combined into 80-character blocks. Another device, such as a CRT, might be able to handle a thousand characters in a record, but the communications line may not tolerate blocks of more than one hundred characters at a time. Figure 7-9 illustrates these examples of blocking and deblocking. The figure also distinguishes between unblocked data, which are data generated by the application, and deblocked data, which are applications data divided up into smaller pieces for the transmission medium.

The second objective is, like that of code conversion, to render the device's physical characteristics as transparent as

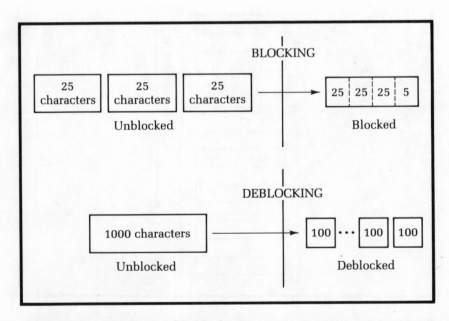

FIGURE 7-9. Blocking and Deblocking

possible to the user or to the user software. Blocking and de-blocking, then, occur in the device-dependent software; if the software blocks a record for a particular device, it must also deblock it for the user software if the device transparency is to be maintained (see Figure 7-10).

Like code conversion, blocking/deblocking is a device-oriented function and is logically on a parallel with code conversion, as shown in Figure 7-11.

Buffering *Buffering* is the process of providing a temporary holding space for records. Our primary interest is in buffers that are used to hold data transmissions before they are processed.

An *input buffer* is a space reserved for an input datum that is to be processed by an applications program, a compiler, or other software process. An *output buffer* is a space reserved for an output datum that is to be transmitted over the communications line. Frequently, a particular activity will require more than one buffer. *Double buffering* is the simplest extension, where two buffers are reserved for the activity. Line printers tend to be double buffered. While one buffer is being emptied by the printer onto the print-line image, the other can be filled from the communications line. Figure 7-12 illustrates this process.

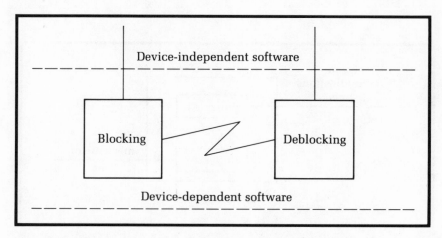

FIGURE 7-10. Device Transparency via Blocking/Deblocking

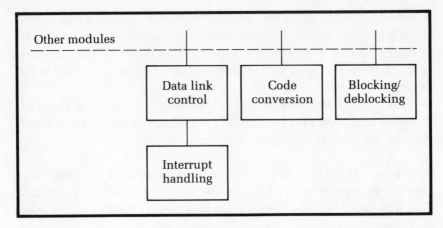

FIGURE 7-11. Data Communications Modules with Blocking/Deblocking

A list consisting of one or more buffers is called a *buffer queue*. Buffer queues are used in a variety of ways in data communications but always to meet one of two objectives. The first objective is to serve as a cushion between two activities that operate at different speeds and in different patterns. For example, an executing program may generate print-line images very quickly, while the printer can only dispatch them relatively slowly. Buffering the lines produced by the applications program permits the applications software to finish and the system to go on with the other work.

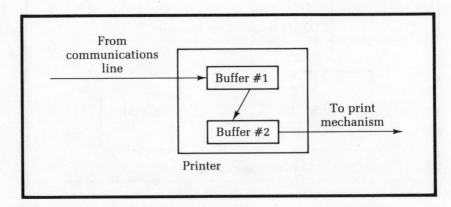

FIGURE 7-12. Printer Double Buffering

The Houston Automatic Spooling Program (HASP) package for IBM 360 and 370 computers is an example of an eminently successful buffering system for both local and remote unit record equipment. Generalized input/output (I/O) buffering systems for unit record equipment are called *spooling systems*.

Data communications systems buffer up, among other things, transmissions to and from terminals. Figure 7-13 shows this use of spooling.

The other objective is to serve as an interface between functions. Here, buffering gives the execution-scheduling function more flexibility by reducing the sizes of the modules

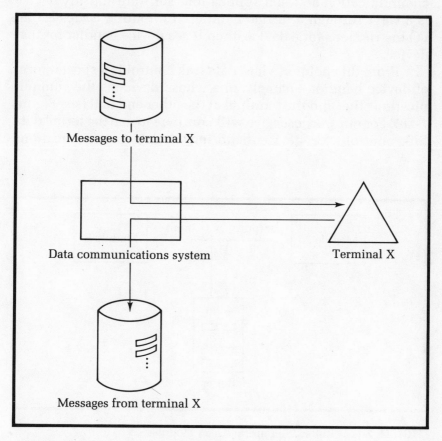

FIGURE 7-13. Buffering To and From Terminals

with which it has to operate. If the interface between two modules is a buffer, as in Figure 7-14, either module can be independently scheduled, assuming that both have input to process. If, however, the interface is a direct subroutine call, then the scheduler must load module B whenever module A is loaded. Figure 7-15 shows this contrasting situation.

Buffering is not restricted to device-oriented functions. Data communications may use buffering as a device-oriented function (Figure 7-16), or it may use buffering in a non-device-oriented way (Figure 7-17).

Device Handling *Device handling* is the software function that interacts directly with the controller for a particular kind of device and, through the controller, controls the device. The communication between applications software and any device is always through a device handler. If a routine issues actual I/O instructions for a device, then it is a device handler for that device.

From this point of view, data link control is a special form of device handler—namely, one whose device is the communications line and the terminal at the other end of it (see Figure 7-18). For our purposes, we will continue to use the term "data link control" for device handling of data communications

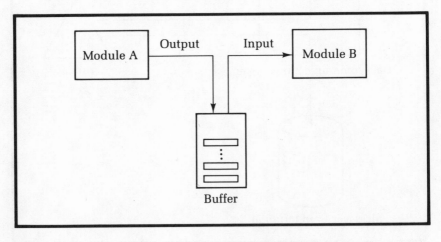

FIGURE 7-14. Buffer Interface Between Modules

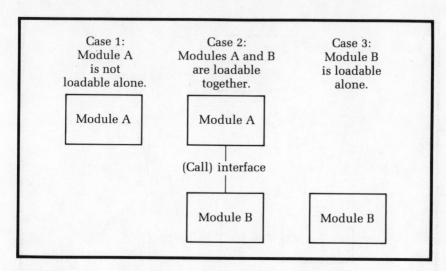

FIGURE 7-15. Load Configurations for Call-Linked Modules

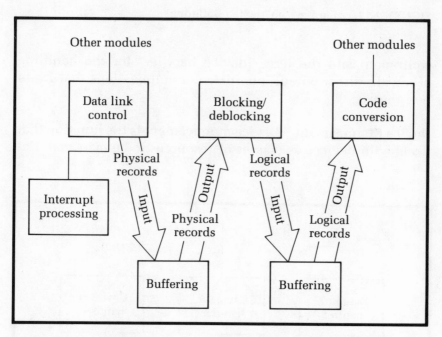

FIGURE   7-16 Device-Oriented Buffering for One Particular Class
of Devices

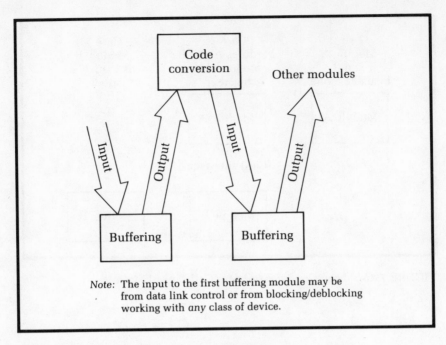

FIGURE 7-17. Non-Device-Oriented Buffering

equipment and the term "device handler" for the handling of local, direct-wired, non-data-communications hardware peripherals.

Device Management *Device management* is the function that deals with devices as classes of resources to be managed. De-

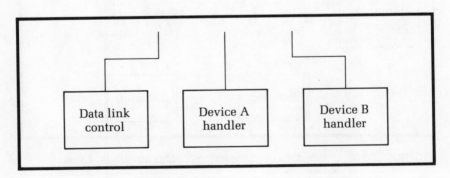

FIGURE 7-18. Device Handlers

vice management translates between the logical requirements of applications software on the one hand and the physical requirements of specific devices on the other hand.

A device manager for the unit record class of devices, for example, accepts card images and line images from an applications program for transmission to a remote terminal. In the process, the device manager converts the card and line images into characters, blocks, or pages (see Figure 7-19).

Device management software has two objectives. First, it relieves applications software of the details of any direct input-output operations, as in the unit record example above. Next, device management makes interchangeability and substitutability of devices possible and completely transparent to the applications software. To provide even greater flexibility, some systems also let device managers communicate with other device managers. Figures 7-20 and 7-21 show how a device manager hooks up to device handlers and to other device managers.

A discussion of device handling and device management is not complete without some mention of file management as well. While device handling deals with traffic intended for a particular device, and device management deals with traffic for a class of devices, *file management* deals with traffic intended for a logical entity called a *file* that may reside on part

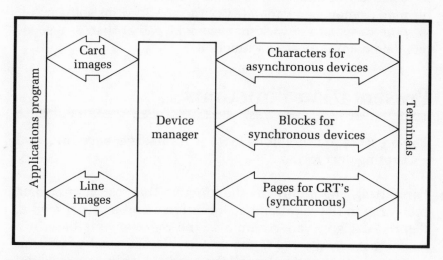

FIGURE 7-19. Device Manager for Unit Record Equipment

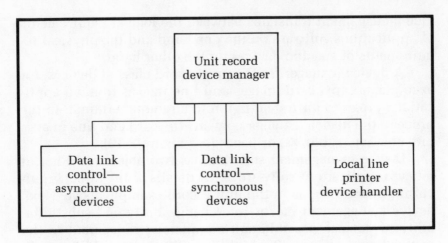

FIGURE 7-20. Device Manager with Interfaces to Device Handlers

of a device or be distributed over several devices. In a data communications system, the file may be on a disk within a remote satellite computer or the file may be separated into pieces residing on equipment scattered throughout an entire network. The latter is called a *distributed data file*. File management translates file-and-record addresses into logical device addresses. Device management translates logical device addresses into physical device addresses. Device handling uses physical device addresses. For our purposes, we will consider file management as a capability of the applications software or, in some cases, of network management, rather than as a separate data communications function.

Presentation Functions

The presentation functions include formatting, encoding, and encrypting/decrypting.

Formatting *Formatting* is the function that restructures data according to the requirements of internal and external media. Figure 7-22 gives an example of the requirements based on media that are internal to the system. Here, a block of data on a communications line has all the trailing blanks squeezed out of it to save transmission time, but the blanks may be added at

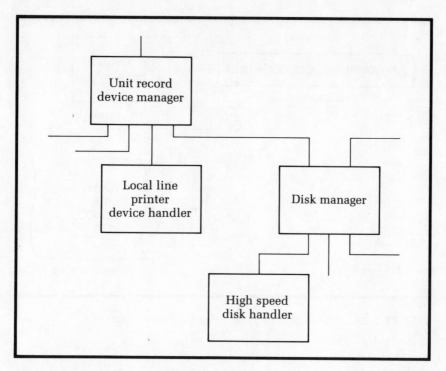

FIGURE 7-21. Device Manager with Interface to Another Device Manager

the end of a line on the printer that receives the transmitted block. In contrast, the formatter may take data that is arranged in one fashion on a disk file and restructure the data to resemble a paperwork form for display on a CRT. Figure 7-23 illustrates this process.

Formatting software has several objectives. First, it allows optimal use of internal media such as computer memory, disk space, and communications lines by providing the necessary routines and algorithms to make the changes in format. Next, it accommodates the unique requirements of external devices such as interactive terminals. It also adapts to the special formats of the data files maintained by various data base management systems (DBMS). Finally, it keeps the reformatting as transparent as possible to the user and to his applications software.

A formatting routine may take output from a computer, for example, and send it out to a line printer as 132-character line images plus page ejects every 60 lines; it can also break the

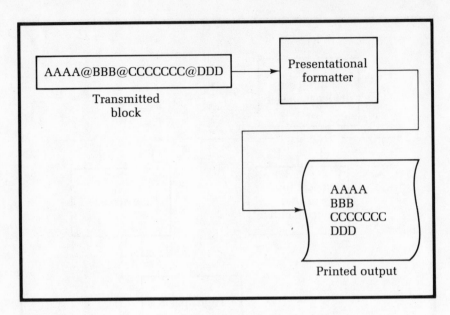

FIGURE 7-22. Presentational Formatting for Printed Output

same output into 72-character lines for a teletype and add the control characters for "carriage return" and "line feed" after every seventy-second character (see Figure 7-24).

Formatting software is usually written as needed, with a different routine for each type of output device. However, generalized "presentation formatting" software can be written so as to draw upon a table of formats according to the type of output device being used (Honeywell, for example, uses such an approach in its network architecture). Since formatting has device-generic input and device-specific output, it is part of the class of system software that has device-generic input and device-specific output. In other words, formatting is a subroutine of device management, as shown in Figure 7-25.

Encoding *Encoding* is the function that converts one datum into another by means of substitution. For example, the datum "MALE" may be converted to the code "1" and "FEMALE" to the code "2." In this sense, encoding is somewhat similar to code conversion. It has, however, the following distinguishing characteristics:

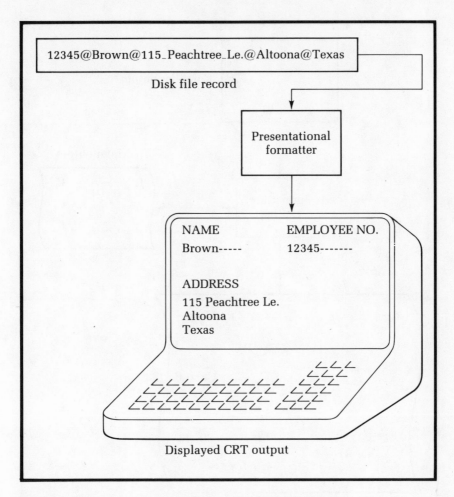

FIGURE 7-23. Presentational Formatting for CRT Output

- Encoding is not necessarily one-to-one. "1 PENN PLAZA" may be converted to the code "52," whereas "@" may be translated into a command meaning "repeat the last message."

- Encoding is at best only positionally unique. For example, the first occurrence of "2" in a message may mean "Acctg. Dept." while the second occurrence may mean "invoice."

- Encoding is dependent on the application, rather than on the device. The example cited above may apply for an

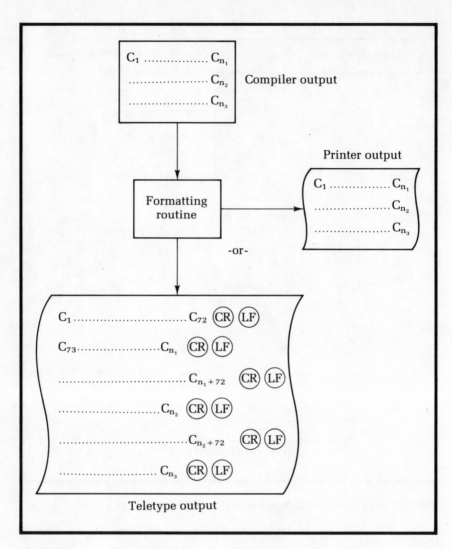

FIGURE 7-24. Device-Generic to Device-Specific Formatting

accounts payable application, but in payroll the first "2" in a message may mean "non-exempt."

Thus, there may be only one code conversion in a data communications system where ASCII terminals are connected to an EBCDIC CPU, but there could be ten different encoding routines, one for each of ten different applications.

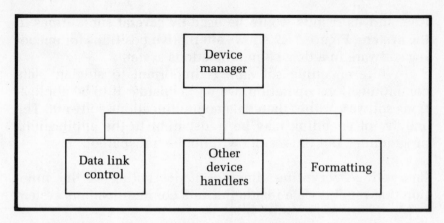

FIGURE 7-25. Formatting Module in Device Manager Subsystem

Figure 7-26 shows how encoding converts back and forth between expanded and condensed forms of data. Encoding routines are generally used to improve line use efficiency by reducing the number of bits that have to be transmitted over the line. Ordinarily, these routines are part of the applications system; however, a well-organized unitary system like a transaction processing system might have only one encoding rou-

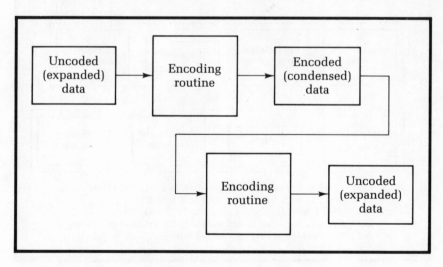

FIGURE 7-26. Operation of the Encoding Function

tine, and its results would be used by several subroutines in the system. Figure 7-27 shows alternative positions for encoding software in a data communications system.

While encoding software is important to efficient data communications operation, we will consider it to be applications software rather than data communications software. The activity of encoding may be transparent to the applications programmer, but the results will not be transparent.

Encrypting/Decrypting *Encrypting/decrypting* is the function that renders data inside the data communications system

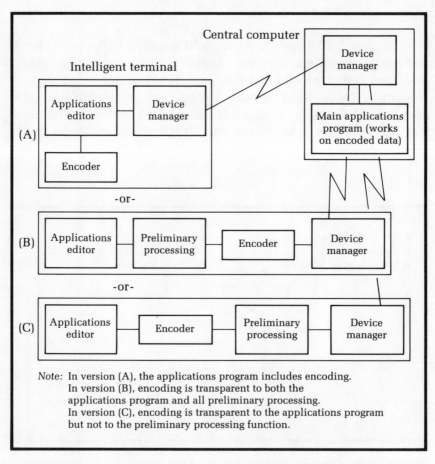

FIGURE 7-27. Alternative Positions for Encoding Functions

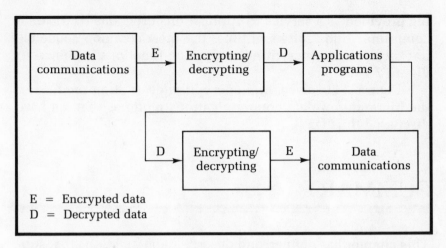

FIGURE 7-28. The Most Common Sequence of Encrypting/Decrypting Functions

secure from unauthorized penetration. This is a process of conversion from one data form to another, using methods similar to but more complicated than those of code conversion. Digital encrypting is a large and important part of data communications technology.

Individual applications may provide their own encrypting routines, employing them in a manner identical to the use of encoding routines. However, it is more common to see encrypt-

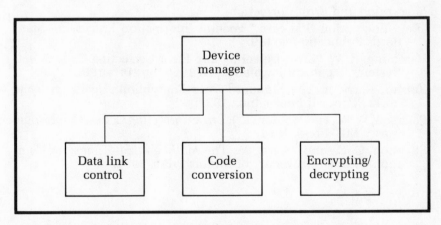

FIGURE 7-29. Organization of Modules Including Encrypting/Decrypting

ing provided as a service to applications programs by the data communications software; thus, the most common sequence of execution for encrypting/decrypting functions is shown in Figure 7-28.

Figure 7-29 places the encrypting/decrypting module in the hierarchy of data communications modules that we have discussed thus far.

SUMMARY

This chapter has defined and described the functions that support hardware operations. These functions may be divided into three separate classes: the line functions, which deal with the communications facilities; the device functions, which deal with a particular terminal; and the presentation functions, which manipulate data for graphic and other packaging requirements. Chapter 8 discusses the software-supporting functions.

REFERENCES

Encryption and Error Correction

"Data Encryption Standard." Federal Information Processing Standards Publication 46 (1977).

Hamming, R. W. "Error Detecting and Error Correcting Codes." Bell Systems Technical Journal, April 1950, pp. 147–160.

Katzan, Harry, Jr. *The Standard Data Encryption Algorithm*. New York: Petrocelli Books, Inc., 1977.

Peterson, W. W., and Weldon, E. J. *Error Correcting Codes*. Cambridge, Mass.: MIT Press, 1972.

Shannon, C. E., and Weaver, W. *The Mathematical Theory of Communications*. University of Illinois Press, 1964.

8

The Software-Supporting Functions

In this chapter we discuss the software-supporting functions introduced in Chapter 6: executive functions, directive functions, quality assurance functions, and intersystem functions.

Executive Functions

The two executive functions, queue management and application servicing, can be discussed at the same time; both affect the sequence in which tasks are accomplished.

Queue management and application servicing are the functions that move data communications message (payload) data around within the environment where the applications software executes. Take, for example, the applications program that totals the individual deposits recorded in each of a series of transactions. In order to maintain a distinction between the data communications software and the applications software and in order to follow successful structured programming techniques, we write the application to handle only the transaction that it sees. Thus, the application program is unaware of the actual number of transactions that are pending and, in particular, of where (in high-speed memory, low-speed memory, or both, or on a distant terminal) they reside.

Queue management keeps track of transactions and moves them along. Except for the fact that queue management also involves queues going to and from terminals, queue management in data communications is exactly like queue management in operating systems. The theory and practice of general queue management is covered very well in texts on operating systems, particularly those by Madnick and Donovan and by Tremblay and Sorenson (see the References section).

Types of Queue Management   Queues may be managed by *first in first out* (FIFO), *last in first out* (LIFO), or *priority* techniques. In message switching, a system that uses only the priority queueing technique must have a natural rhythm for purging the system. If the system does not have a purging rhythm, then it needs "automatic promotion" (automatic change of priority). Any system that has fewer priority levels than messages must also have FIFO or LIFO built into the scheduling of queues.

Queue management and the services it provides to applications, such as delivering or accepting a queue entry, should be separated from the actual queue being managed. A system may have many queues (for such elements as messages in, messages out, applications programs to be run), yet its queue management techniques are limited to the trio just mentioned—FIFO, LIFO, and priority.

Figure 8-1 shows the queues typical of a timesharing system. An abbreviated list of queues in a data communications system is shown in Figure 8-2.

In some systems where data communications is added after the operating system is built, queue management will already exist for the basic system functions such as fast-memory allocation and program execution. In this case, only data communications (or message) queue management need be added (see Figure 8-3).

Since queue management avoids direct subroutine calls, it can facilitate "simultaneous" and "asynchronous" execution

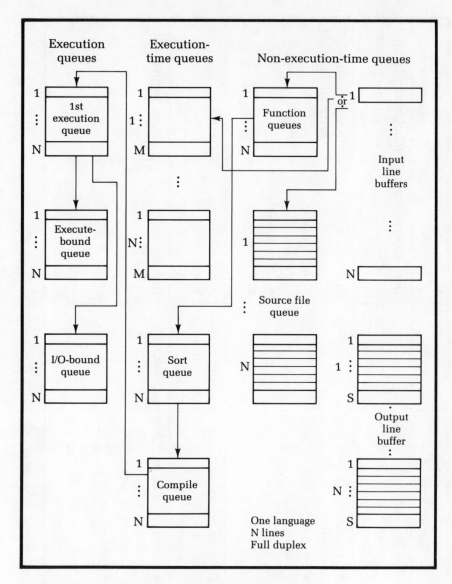

FIGURE 8-1. Major Queues in a Timesharing System

of modules. Queue managers can be generalized to work with various parameters. The execution queue, for example, can contain all that is necessary for the executive to find a particular module, start it in execution, and then terminate it after a unit of time has expired—this unit also being one of the parameters.

Queue name	Contents	Inserted by:	Removed by:	Function performed
Input queue (message queue)	Message with header and trailers	DLC	Device management	Blocking/deblocking Sorting into process queues
Process queue (message queue)	• Messages to be output • Transaction for same process	Device management	Process module • Device management output • Other module • Transaction processing	The work of the particular module
Execution queue (function queue)	Pointers to process modules to be executed	Scheduler or device management	• Scheduler • Executive	Activation
Disk queue—output (device queue)	• Pointer to data in memory with location on disk • Data (if transaction processing) and file location	File management	Disk handler	Written to disk

FIGURE 8-2. Examples of Queues Maintained in a Data Communications System

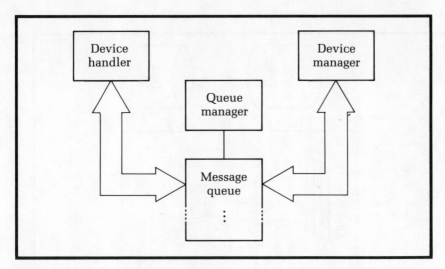

FIGURE 8-3. Queue Manager for Data Communications Messages

Directive Functions

The directive functions include transaction scheduling and processing, resource management, and network management.

Transaction Scheduling and Processing *Transaction scheduling and processing* is the function that decides which queues should hold which transactions—sometimes a problem of matching up transaction codes with table names, sometimes one of reassigning transaction codes as transactions emerge from processes and then matching them up. Sometimes the same module both schedules and processes the transactions. Sometimes the scheduling module is reentrant; sometimes the module would have to be too knowledgeable of the sequence of transactions to be as independent of them as reentrancy requires.

Figure 8-4 shows scheduling as performed by a transaction scheduler (part A) and indicates representative transaction processes (part B). These processes could service such varied applications as line-by-line compilers or passbook accounting programs for banks.

Transaction scheduling can just as easily be a batch operation as a data communications function. In fact, some data communications systems, such as timesharing and remote

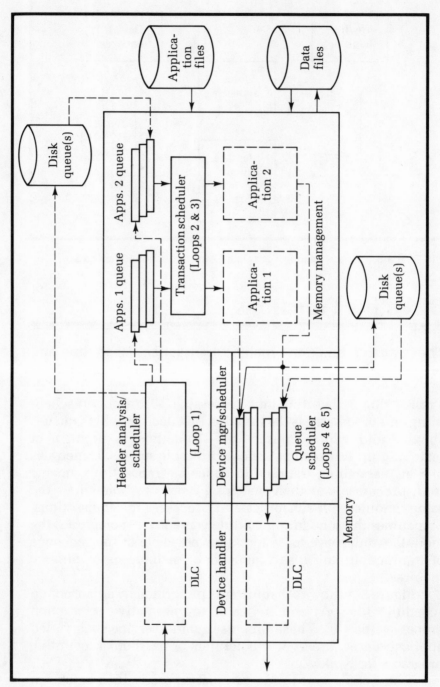

FIGURE 8-4 (Part A). Scheduling in a Transaction Processing System

batch, need not include any transaction processing at all. For those cases where the data communications system does use transaction processing, Figure 8-5 shows its relationship to other data communications modules.

Resource Management *Resource management* is a function that keeps track of the various system media and facilities, such as the primary fast memory, the compilers, and the remote

---

Loop 1: Header analysis scheduler
1. Receives transaction from I/O control system data/ device manager
2. Sorts transaction into queue for appropriate module

Loop 2: Transaction Scheduler
1. Checks for empty space in memory (or for free initiator)
2. Searches for nonempty input queue
3. Activates (or loads) appropriate module

Loop 3: Transaction scheduler
1. Looks for input queue overflow condition or aging criteria met
2. Forces empty space (or quiescent module)
3. Loop 2, step 3

Loop 4: Queue scheduler
1. Looks for output queue overflow
2. Forces quiescence

Loop 5: Queue scheduler
1. Receives output transaction from all modules
2. Hands over to I/O control (device manager) for sorting in lines

Note: Module (or process application) works on queue until queue is empty or the module is forced quiescent. However, if module is reentrant, the queue is actively controlled by Loop 2 and the module is "called" for each entry.

FIGURE 8-4 (Part B). Scheduling in a Transaction Processing System

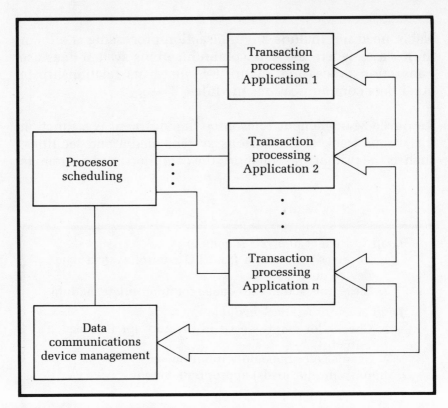

FIGURE 8-5. Relationship of Transaction Processing to Data Communications Modules

terminals, as resources to be allocated to users. Indeed, almost everything in a complex system can be considered a resource. Some analyses of operating systems consider the entire system to be a resource manager (see the text by Madnick and Donovan listed in the References section). Figure 8-6 lists some of the resources in a typical data communications system.

There is a natural relationship among queue managers, transaction scheduler/processors, and resource managers. Figure 8-7 shows a typical situation. Here, the transaction processor decides which transaction to process, the memory resource manager decides how to allocate or deallocate memory, and the queue manager carries out the mechanics of queueing and dequeueing.

1. Hardware resources
   - Links (lines between two nodes)
   - Terminals or terminal clusters
   - Nodes (communication processors, concentrators, front end processors)
   - General purpose computers
   - Disks
   - Memory

2. Software Resources
   - Work files
   - Data files
   - Applications modules
   - Compilers, assemblers, system utilities
   - DLC's (device handlers)
   - I/O managers (device managers)
   - Load modules (including downline modules— those sent from a main computer to a remote computer)
   - Operating systems
   - Schedulers
   - Queues

These resources are allocated according to:
- Priority of message (or process) needing resource
- Time of arrival of message
- Relationship to other messages (e.g., transaction processing)

Their allocation is changed as:
- Resources are freed up
- New requirements appear
- Backup is needed

FIGURE 8-6. Resources in a Typical Data Communications System

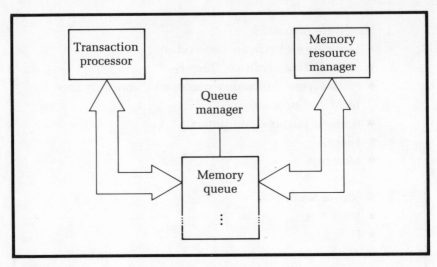

FIGURE 8-7. The Relationships Among a Queue Manager, Transaction Processor, and Resource Manager

Network Management *Network management* is the function that keeps track of the various network facilities and implements the strategies by which they are utilized. Typical network entities that may be tracked are indicated in Figure 8-8. These physical entities include devices, lines, and facilities such as remote batch. When these facilities are combined into logical entities, allocation is made in terms of the new logical pieces—in terms of *paths*, for instance, rather than data links.

- Data links
- Terminals
- Communications processors
- Host computers
- Data storage facilities
- Computational facilities
- Applications subsystems
- Applications support facilities

FIGURE 8-8. Network Resources

(A *path* is a route from one point to another. It may include any number of data links.)

In a hierarchical network (Figure 8-9) and in a star-shaped network (Figure 8-10), one computer is dominant and all resources are allocated from that central computer. Centralized control is natural to a hierarchical or star network. Resources may also be interlinked and allocated at each end, and there may be intermediate resource allocations on a volunteer, or *gossip*, basis, as in the ARPAnet example in Figure 8-11.

Every network management activity can be broken down into resource management tasks such as the following:

- Selection of a path for the message

- Selection of an alternate destination for the message

- Deactivation (physically or logically) of the terminal or intermediate node

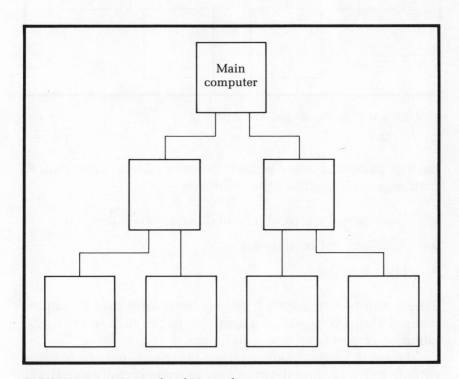

FIGURE 8-9.   A Hierarchical Network

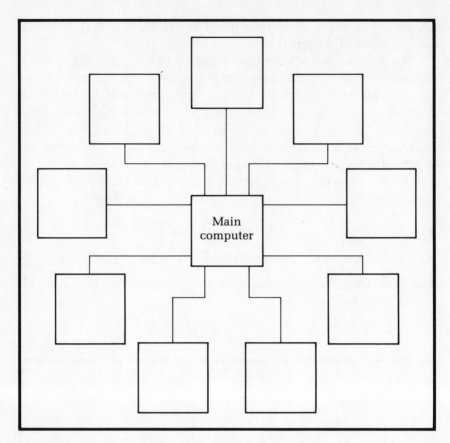

FIGURE 8-10. A Star-Shaped Network

Each of these tasks may be further broken down; for instance, path selection considers the following:

- Operational status of terminals and nodes involved
- Avoidance of bottlenecks
- Load leveling

These examples of network management tasks may be implemented through queue management techniques, even if the parameters vary from queue to queue.

Network management requires no special data communications software since network management is really a separate

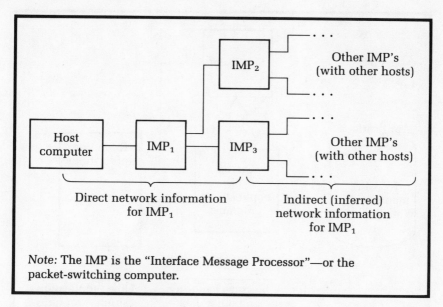

FIGURE 8-11. ARPAnet-style Network Information

applications program in one or more computers. It generates messages and inquiries to carry out its work by using the data communications facilities in its hosts; it calls on system monitoring, error recovery, device management, network configuration control, polling and callings, and queue management functions, as shown in Figure 8-12.

Quality Assurance Functions

The quality assurance functions include systems monitoring and self-testing, interactive debugging, archiving, and journaling.

Systems Monitoring, Self-Testing, and Interactive Debugging *Systems monitoring, self-testing, and interactive debugging* are the functions of the data communications system concerned with its internal workings. Systems monitoring is the function that observes and records data about the data com-

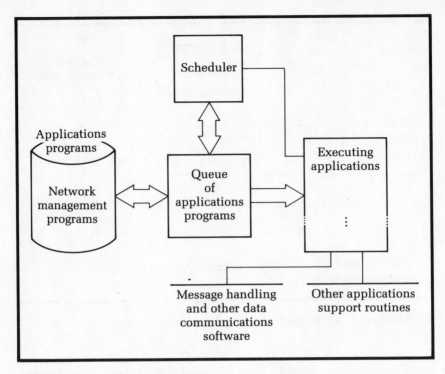

FIGURE 8-12. Relationship of Network Management to Other Data Communications Software

munications system while the system is operating. Figure 8-13 shows examples of its monitoring.

Self-testing is the function that exercises other functions of the data communications system so that their operations can be verified and measured. Typical examples include:

- *Ghost programs* that exercise the compilers, schedulers, and I/O functions of timesharing

- *Round-robin messages* that exercise the message-switching functions

- *Probes of distant terminals* that exercise the link protocols

Figure 8-14 shows the relationship of self-testing software to the rest of the system. Notice that self-testing software looks like applications software to the system. A status checker like the one in Farber's ring system is an example of a self-testing software function.

Interactive debugging software permits the user to inspect parts of the memory of the system and to revise the system's operation in an "on-line" fashion. Interactive debugging software also looks like applications software to the system. It differs from self-testing software in that interactive debugging occasionally has to have special privileges in order to display the system's own queues of buffers and the contents of system tables and work areas.

Interactive debugging aids date back at least to the days of the first keyboard-type operator's consoles. A special feature used for data communications is the ability to insert messages into the data communications stream in order to force certain responses from the system. Interactive debugging of traffic flow to and from distant terminals is accomplished by letting the interactive debugging terminal function as a normal terminal. This sometimes requires additional flexibility in assigning devices. The console chosen is often the CPU's console, and the debugging function may not even use the I/O controller.

The repertoire of software routines available for interactive debugging is quite extensive. Each debugging routine is grouped loosely into a subsystem of applications modules. Examples of interactive debugging include the following:

- Displaying contents of individual messages

- Counting message traffic

- Activating/deactivating error-checking modules

Archiving and Journaling   *Archiving and journaling* are the data communications functions that act like cameras, taking pictures of the activities of the data communications system. To carry the analogy further, we can say that archiving functions make running documentaries while journaling functions take isolated snapshots of data communications activities.

Archiving software makes permanent copies of major portions of data bases. A routine practice of timesharing systems, for example, is that of making a daily copy of each user's data files. A typical timesharing system, such as General Electric's Mark III, might make a copy each day of each file and retain

	Component	Condition	How Checked
Software	Terminal	Connected up	Polling
		Hung up	Count WACK's (wait acknowledgments) in interval
		Malfunctioning	Count in/out NAK's (negative acknowledgments)
	Line (DL)	Quality	NAK's, especially if multidrop
	Communication processor	Connected up	Polling/hand shaking (protocol initiation)
	Intelligent terminal or minis	Connected up	Polling/hand shaking
		Functional	Handshake in downline load
	Disk/tape reader/printer	Functional	Controller status indicator (byte)

Component		Condition	How Checked
Hardware	Application	Functional	Verify output generated (time-out) Input queue untouched
		Malfunctioning	Hardware instruction check Memory protect/page violation Write request on read file
	Compiler or Utility	Malfunctioning —same as above plus—	Exceeding maximum memory request Exceeding maximum time allowed Failure to compile/benchmark (QA programs)
	General	Malfunctioning	Failure to make time, data, output criteria in QA "ghost"
	Operating system	Self-functioning	QA by kernel (resident portion of operating system) on request for allowed services
		Parallel functioning	Parallel operation of certain functions plus periodic interrogation/response cycles

FIGURE 8-13. Examples of System Monitoring

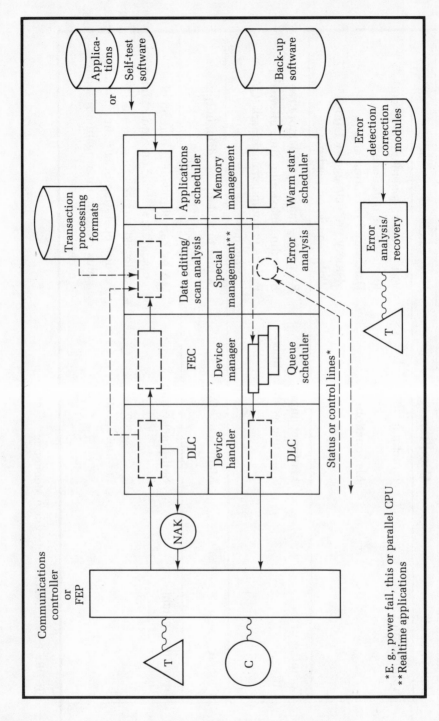

FIGURE 8-14. Relationship of Self-Testing Software to the Data Communications System

those files for a month. After one month, only weekly tapes might be retained (for example, only the Saturday tapes). After six months, only the monthly tapes might be retained, and these are kept for up to two years.

This archiving activity makes it possible to reconstruct vital files after an error occurs. The error may be caused by the application software or by the operating system. Applications errors are more likely to affect the active files—hence the importance of keeping the daily tapes for several weeks. Inactive files are subject primarily to system failure. They can often be restored from a prior month without any disruption to the user's application.

Journaling software makes copies of individual transactions. This frequently is done on magnetic tape because disks are too busy. For protection, such a tape will be appended to but never rewound or rewritten. Journaled data may include any of the following:

- A system-unique transaction number
- The name of the software module or network node receiving the transaction
- The time of arrival at that node
- The time transmitted out of that node
- Contents of the transaction

In high-volume systems, the transaction contents might be scaled down to a simple count of characters in a message. Also the journaling function might copy only a sample of the transactions rather than an entire set.

Journaled data provide all of the following:

- A dynamic pattern of system inputs, outputs, and throughput
- A data base of real transactions that can be used to exercise the system
- A data base of real transactions that will serve to model the system when a new network is proposed

Both the archiving functions and the journaling functions are utilities as far as the other data communications modules are concerned. They are invoked periodically, as established by the schedule or recording philosophy of the system (see Figure 8-15).

Intersystem Functions

The intersystem functions include error recovery and the operating system interface.

Error Recovery *Error recovery* functions are of many different types, invoked under many different circumstances. Figure 8-16 gives examples of these functions. Error recovery functions are utilities to data communications functions such as network management and to data link control.

Operating System Interface The *operating system interface* function is a loose collection of software modules that request, use, and restore services provided by the operating system. All

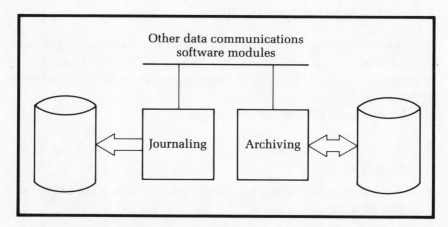

FIGURE 8-15. Relationship of Archiving and Journaling Functions to Other Data Communications Modules

Error	Error Recovery Function
Loss of dedicated line	Reroute traffic to dial-up (switched) line
Failure of applications software module	Fall back to more limited and safer version
Parity error/CRC (cyclic redundancy check) failure	Forward error correction or retransmit (ARQ)
Failure of link	Reroute messages around the data link
Failure of network mode	Reroute to other nodes or hold till operational
CPU fails	Dual processor takes up workload

FIGURE 8-16. Examples of Error Recovery Functions

of these modules are called by the other modules that carry out the unique work of data communications, as shown in Figure 8-17.

Interface Functions	Data Communications Module Using the Service
Disk I/O	Disk queueing in message switching
High speed (primary) memory management	Queue management
Applications scheduling	Transaction scheduler

FIGURE 8-17. Operating System Interface Functions for Data Communications

SUMMARY

In this chapter, we have examined the software-supporting functions. They are divided into classes—executive functions, directive functions, quality assurance functions, and intersystem functions. The various functions in each of these classes were explained here in familiar programming terms. In Chapter 9 we will see how these functions support specific applications.

REFERENCES

Network Management

Schwartz, Boorstyn, and Pickholtz. "Terminal-Oriented Computer-Communications Networks." IEEE 60 (November 1972).

Operating Systems

Braden. "Operating Systems." In *Computer Science*, edited by Cardenas et al., 1972.

Holt, Graham, Lazowska, and Scott. *Structured Concurrent Programming with Operating Systems Applications*. Reading, Mass.: Addison-Wesley, 1978.

Madnick, Stuart E., and Donovan, John J. *Operating Systems*. New York: McGraw-Hill, 1974.

Queue Management

Kleinrock, L. *Queueing Systems*. New York: John Wiley and Sons, vol. 1 (1975), vol. 2 (1976).

Kleinrock, L. *Communication Nets*. New York: McGraw-Hill, 1964.

9

Organization of the Software Functions to Support Particular Applications

This chapter shows how the functions described in Chapter 8 are used to build or to provide a foundation for the specific applications of data communications. The applications we discuss are message switching, remote job entry, timesharing information retrieval, online update, and transaction processing.

Message Switching

The fundamental responsibility of message-switching software is to read a message from one terminal and write that message to another terminal, as illustrated in Figure 9-1. In a mailbox type of message-switching system, there is one input buffer for each terminal and one output buffer for each terminal (see

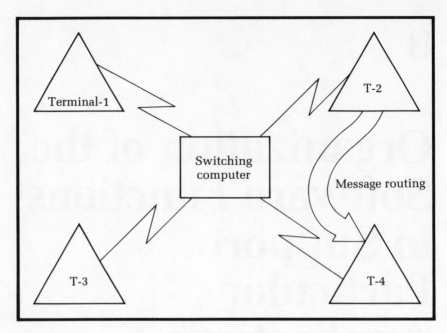

FIGURE 9-1. Message Switching

Figure 9-2). In such a system, if the terminals are identical, no software is needed other than data link control and header analysis software. Data link control handles the communications line. The header analysis software identifies the receiving terminal and places the message in the appropriate output "mailbox."

The ARPAnet is a type of packet-switching network. Its communications processors are not generalized for a variable number of communications lines. Instead, they have an input buffer for each incoming line, and they write their messages out of that buffer onto the appropriate outgoing line (see Figure 9-3). Accomplishing this complete task requires only data link control for input, header analysis for routing, and data link control for output.

Message-Switching Extensions If there is not a one-to-one correspondence between incoming and outgoing lines in a message-switching system, outgoing messages for particular lines may accumulate faster than they can be dispatched. To handle such cases, a queue of buffers is required for each line.

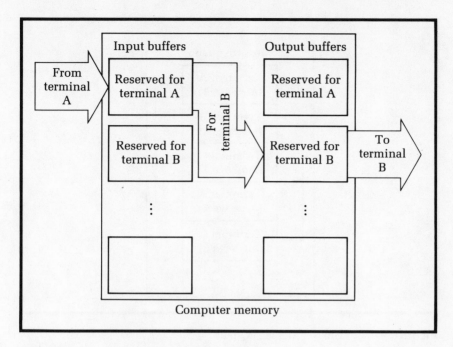

FIGURE 9-2. A Mailbox Switching System

Alternatively, a single buffer queue shared by all the lines must exist so that any given line can have several messages pending at one time. Figure 9-4 shows such a message queue. These extensions permit a message-switching system to deal with a

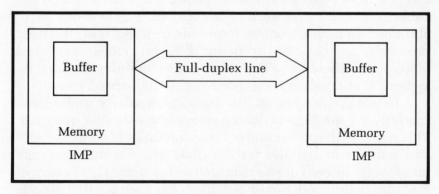

FIGURE 9-3. ARPAnet Switching Between Two Interface Message Processors (IMP's) on a Data Link

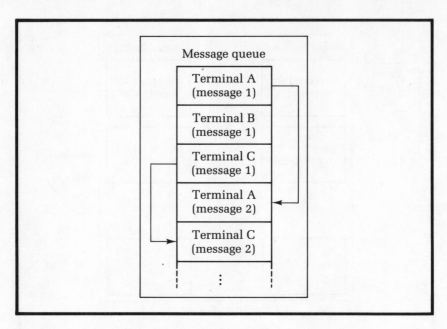

FIGURE 9-4. A Shared Message Queue

variable-demand workload. In such cases, the header analysis module becomes a queue manager. All the necessary software for message switching is shown in Figure 9-5.

Other extensions to the message-switching system include code conversion between terminals of different types, which is handled by the queue manager (see Figure 9-6) and speed conversion between terminals of different types, which is accomplished by using more than one data link control module. Other conversions between terminals, such as between asynchronous and synchronous terminals or those with different protocols, are handled by using different data link control modules, as shown in Figure 9-7. These modules are used by systems that do all of their queueing in high-speed memory.

To deal with very erratic loads, particularly under peak conditions, a message-switching system may add disk queueing. This requires the additional software modules of a file manager and a driver or handler for the disk. The file manager may incorporate its own queue management system. This system of modules is shown in Figure 9-8. Such a system is called a *core-disk switching system.*

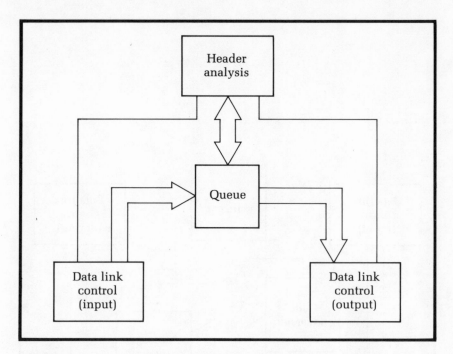

FIGURE 9-5. Essential Software Modules for Message Switching

Remote Job Entry

A remote entry system permits users to insert batch jobs at remote card reader batch stations and to receive the output from those jobs at remote printers and card punches (usually the same batch stations). As in message-switching systems, data link control is required for input and output.

Necessary Modules We can identify the other necessary modules by following the course of a job through the system. An incoming job passes from data link control into a memory buffer. The memory buffer is controlled by a software module called a *symbiont*, whose responsibility it is to insert the incoming job into the job stream on the disk (see Figure 9-9). In today's large-scale remote job entry systems, the central computer is a multiprogrammed computer and has a complex job input queue on its disk. Such a queue may be served from several local card readers. A module called the *reader* is re-

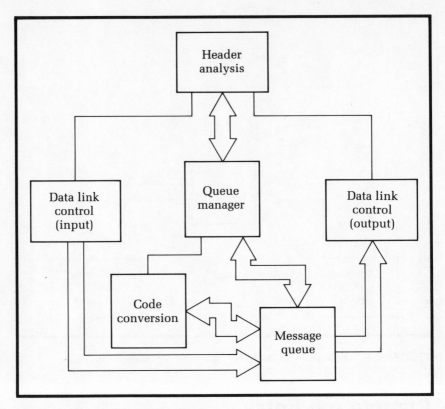

FIGURE 9-6. Message-Switching Modules with Code Conversion

sponsible for reading jobs from the various local card readers and placing them onto the disks. The symbiont does the same thing, but it uses as its source a remote card reader rather than a local card reader.

If the remote job entry system is superimposed upon an existing multiprogrammed system, the symbiont is added to the reader as an extension. The reader proceeds to put the incoming job onto the disk, using the file manager and the disk handler modules. Later these modules are used in reverse by the *initiator*, a module that executes the incoming job after removing it from a disk. The normal *batch executive* monitors the program in execution, and the *output writer* places line image messages on the disk using the file manager and disk driver software. Then the output writer, expanded by the out-

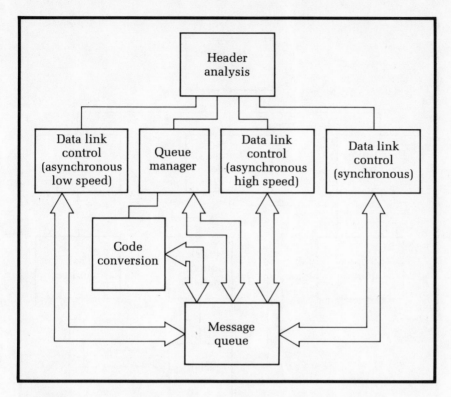

FIGURE 9-7. Message Switching with Various Data Link Controls

put symbiont, reads the line images from the disk and writes them through data link control onto the output remote job entry printer or cardpunch. Examples of such systems include Sigma-9's CP-5 operating systems and IBM's RJE and HASP systems.

Sometimes the system's RJE services are destination-restricted. This permits only those jobs originating at a given remote job entry terminal to be returned to that terminal. In destination-restricted systems, the input symbiont marks the input job, and the output symbiont, after checking that mark, uses data link control to select the proper output terminal. In more flexible systems, the job control language (JCL) is modified to permit selection of a variable output station and multiple copies of the same job through repeated printings of the output file.

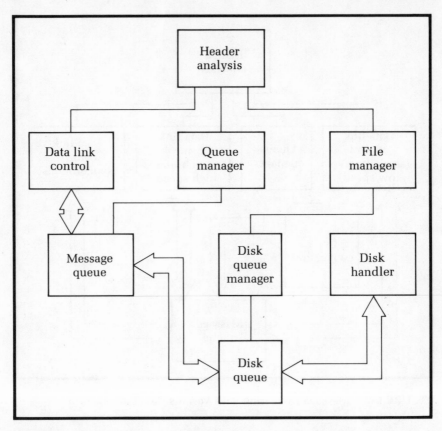

FIGURE 9-8. Message Switching with Core-Disk Queueing

Timesharing

The principal function of a timesharing system is to provide interactive execution to a user at a remote keyboard terminal. In a timesharing system, the user has the impression that he or she has sole use of the computer; however, through the use of a time-slicing mechanism, several users can execute their programs simultaneously. *Time-slicing* means that each unit of time is cut up into several pieces. A "slice" of CPU time is given alternately to each user of the system. Switching between the various programs is done very rapidly so that the program appears to the user to be executing continuously.

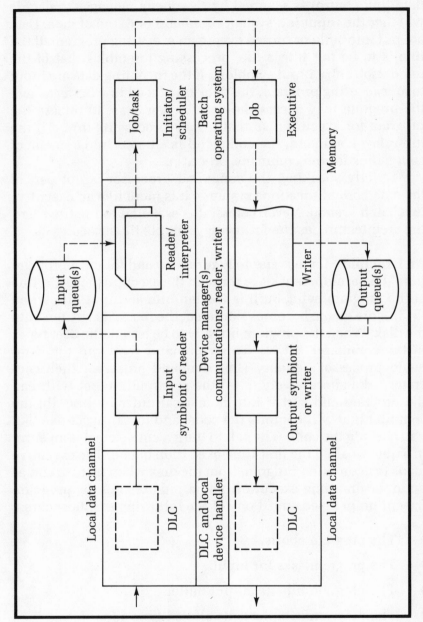

FIGURE 9-9. Remote Job Entry Architecture

In a timesharing system, each line typed by the user is treated separately. A line coming into the system through data link control is scanned by the queue manager to decide whether the input is a system command or a line of data. Data are put into a file or turned over to an executing program. If the line is to be put into a file, processing resembles that of the remote job entry input symbiont. If the incoming data are input to an executing program, the data are placed in a buffer where the program may access the data. A flag is set to release the program for execution so that it may process its input. If the input is a command, the command is entered into a queue of commands for the command processor.

Strictly speaking, the command processor is not part of the data communications system—it is more like an executive in a batch system. Nevertheless, it is essential to the timesharing architecture, as the following example illustrates.

An Example Let us refer to Figure 9-10 and follow a program from the development stage through the execution stage. A line of the program being built is written into an input file. When the in-core queue becomes saturated, the record is written onto the disk. When the program is ready to be tested, the user types in the command "RUN." This command goes into the command processor's queue. The command processor then generates calls successively to (a) the sort routine that will read the program and sort it into numerical order by line, (b) the compiler that will compile the code, and (c) the executive that will execute the code. The call to the executive creates an entry in a queue called the first-time-execution queue. The executive loads the compiled program from the disk when its turn comes up in the first-time-execution queue and executes the program. Execution proceeds until one of the following events occurs:

- The program aborts.

- The program asks for input.

- The program fills its output buffer.

- The program completes its alloted time slice.

The Three-Queue Strategy Timesharing uses a "three-queue strategy" to give the appearance that the computer is solely at

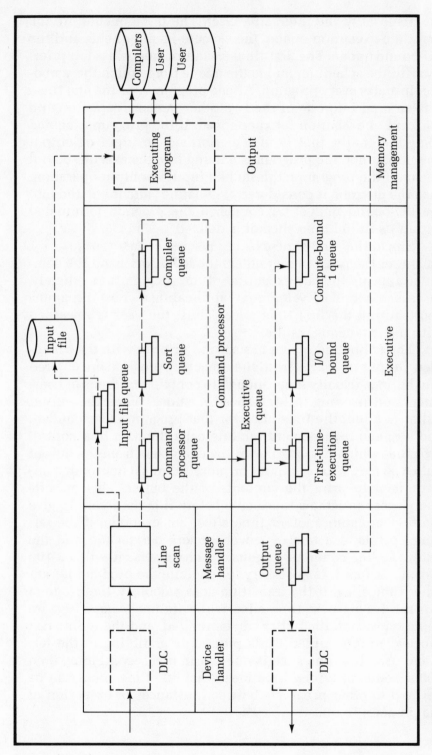

FIGURE 9-10. Timesharing System Architecture Showing User Program and Command Flow

the disposal of the interactive user. The three queues are the first-time-execution queue, the execute-bound queue, and the I/O-bound queue. The first-time-execution queue has top priority with the scheduler and is the queue from which the scheduler initiates every program. After a program runs the first time, it is entered into one of the two other queues, depending on the kind of execution it experienced. If the program executed computationally, that is, if it performed no input or output operation, then the program is entered into the execute-bound queue. If the program requested an input or output operation, then the program is considered "I/O-bound" and is entered into the I/O-bound queue. Of course, if the program terminated within its initial time slice, it is deleted.

Since the first-time-execution queue has top priority, whenever the programmer enters the RUN command the computer appears to start execution of the program immediately. In research and development applications, most programs abort during the first time slice. Thus, the user is rewarded with instantaneous results.

The I/O-bound queue has second priority with the scheduler. Output messages from the executing program are entered into buffers, usually large enough to contain hundreds of characters and residing in high-speed memory. When the output buffer is filled, the time slice for that program is suspended, and a queue management module calls the data link control program, which begins to print the characters from the output buffer. It may take a minute or more in an asynchronous environment to print the contents of the buffer. This permits many other programs to execute before it is necessary to give the first program another time slice. For example, if the terminal prints at a rate of ten characters per second and the output buffer contains a thousand characters, it will be 100 seconds before it is necessary to schedule the program for another time slice. If the transition goes smoothly, the program can receive its next time slice while its final characters are being typed out, the buffer can be refilled, and the typing can proceed uninterrupted. This process is gratifying to the terminal user. If a time slice is one-fourth of a second long, then 100 seconds of typing time mean that 400 time slices can be devoted to other programs between instances of execution of the program in question.

The third queue is the execute-bound queue. A program that does not do any input or output in its last time slice is consigned to this queue. These programs have third priority; they are given only occasional time slices, but in some cases their time slices are longer than those that other programs get. They are essentially space fillers for other programs. An execute-bound program, then, appears to execute very slowly, but since that is exactly what the user expects, user confidence in the timesharing system is maintained.

Recent Developments   The structure of timesharing systems has remained relatively constant since the days of the Dartmouth BASIC System of Kemeny and Kertz. Contemporary examples include the General Electric Mark III timesharing system and IBM's "Time-Sharing Option" (TSO) under its OS and VS operating systems. Many manufacturers of modern minicomputers offer timesharing systems that are similarly constructed; Digital Equipment Corporation's RSX-11 software is one example.

Recent advances in compilers and languages make very efficient use of the input and output facilities. The limiting factor in such systems tends to be not the communication but the primary and secondary memory of the computer. The size of the primary memory limits the number of programs that can be maintained simultaneously in memory. It is faster to switch from one program to another in memory than it is to "roll out" a program and "roll in" another one. Similarly, it is faster to get the program compiled if the compiler is memory-resident than if the compiler has to be read from secondary storage.

A compiler can be more efficiently used if that compiler is reentrant; reentrancy makes it possible for a single copy of the compiler to work on several programs simultaneously. If the compiler generates reentrant compiled code, additional time savings are achieved because it will not be necessary to roll out the whole program after each time slice. While the entire program must be rolled in from memory, only the variable parts need to be rolled out. Since reentrant code does not change, the version of the program that is on the disk can be used over and over again until the program terminates.

Information Retrieval

Information retrieval networks exist for the purpose of searching data bases and providing answers to users at keyboard terminals. A retrieval system may be considered the equivalent of a timesharing system that has only one compiler and no execution stage. All inputs coming from terminals are entered into queues where they are examined by the information retrieval program. The information retrieval program treats inquiries as transactions to be processed against a data base.

Since the retrieval software may be quite complex (and for our purposes may be considered to be applications code), we need concern ourselves only with the structure of the non-search software. That software consists of (a) data link control, (b) message analysis, which is like a queue management function, and (c) the printing function implemented through the output queue manager and the output data link control (see Figure 9-11). Examples of information retrieval systems include the New York Times Infobank and the National Institute of Health's MEDLINE.

Online Update

The purpose of an online update system is to permit a user operating at a remote terminal to alter the contents of a data base at the central computer. The flow of control is as follows:

- User inputs data through data link control to the queue handler.

- The update application receives the input message from the queue handler.

- The applications program obtains the appropriate record from the disk.

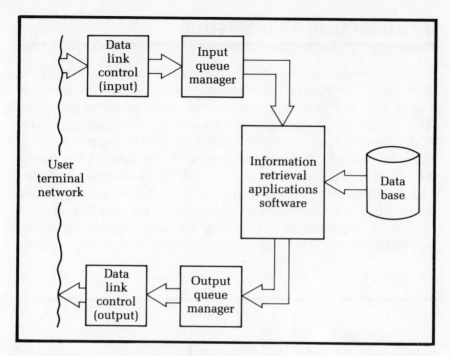

FIGURE 9-11. The Data Communications Software of Information Retrieval

- The applications program makes the required modification to the record.

- The applications program sends the modified record back to the disk.

- The applications program places an acknowledgment message with the output queue scheduler. The applications queue scheduler turns the message over to data link control for output.

The sequence of modules in online update is equivalent to the sequence of modules used for information retrieval with the additional capability of changing the data base. Figure 9-11, then, illustrates the basic set of modules for online update except that the data flow both ways between the applications module and the data base.

Transaction Processing

The purpose of transaction processing is to impose a data structure discipline upon a network application so that the processing of data for that application is as economical as possible. The functions of transaction processing are information retrieval and online update. However, transaction processing is oriented toward CPU and realtime economy through the use of highly encoded fixed message formats for both input and output. Information retrieval and online update, on the other hand, tend to be more flexible with their message formats.

Some transaction processing systems employ reentrant applications modules and a sophisticated applications sched-

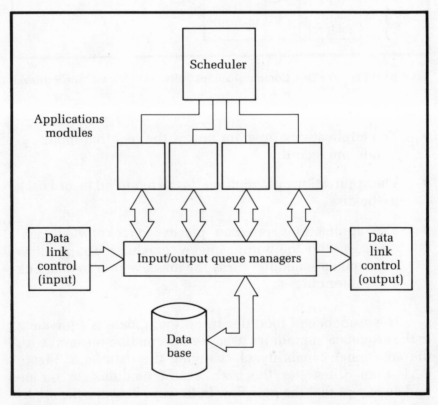

FIGURE 9-12. The Data Communications Software of Transaction Processing

uler to maximize efficient processing throughout. A generalized transaction processing system is outlined in Figure 9-12.

SUMMARY

This chapter has described and explained the general classes of network applications. It has shown how these application types are built upon the functions that we have examined in earlier chapters.

10

Mixing Data and Control (META) Information

This chapter introduces the concept of metadata, or data about data. We discuss three different types of metadata: information data, message control information, and network control information.

Information or Text Data

The information or *text data* in a message is the payload content of that message—in other words, it is the information for whose transmission the network was built in the first place.

Inventory control networks send such information as the quantity on hand, the price per unit, the quantity ordered, and the shipping weight. Airlines reservations systems send such information as passenger name, intermediate and final destinations, and type of accommodation required. Theater reservations networks send the seat numbers of available seats and the names and seat numbers of those who purchased tickets. Text processing systems send the letters of abbreviation of each word and the codes for symbols that are used to control typesetting of a phrase, paragraph, or page.

A *payload message* is one that contains payload data. We can say that payload messages are the elements with which the applications of the network operate. In the preceding examples the applications were obvious—inventory control, airlines reservations, theater reservations, and text processing. The applications in message-switching systems are less obvious; one application is the "read message" application, the other is the "send message" application (in other words, read and print).

Source and Destination   In data communications systems there are several physical sources of data. For message switching, data originate at the transmitting terminal. For remote job entry, although the jobs to be executed originate at the input terminal, the completed jobs originate at the data center computer. In such systems, the destination as well as the source must be made known at the data center so that completed jobs can be sent to the appropriate terminals. The source is implicit; the destination must be made explicit. It must be recorded in the message or attached to the message by data communications software. The alternative is to write special logic, for each input terminal, in the data communications package at the central site. This is tolerable for a small number of terminals (two, perhaps) but not for a larger number.

Inventory control, airlines reservations, theater reservations, and text processing systems are all representative of online information retrieval (*inquiry response*) systems. The source of query information is the terminal; the source of response data is the data base at the data center computer. In such systems, the destination is implicit; destination and origin are the same.

Data Structures   There are other characteristics of interest in data besides the data themselves and their sources and destinations. These characteristics are the *data structures*—the form and organization of the data. In some systems the structure is part of the data. Most often the data structure is conveyed in message control information, which is the subject of the next section.

Examples of data that contain their own elements of data structure appear in systems where the applications format their own data, such as in variable-length fields of multifield records. These applications insert count fields or field separators in the data in order to delimit data elements within fields and to delimit data fields within records. Figures 10-1 and 10-2 illustrate the use of field identifiers, length counters, and field separators.

As the reader can see from the terminology used in this section, the word *record* is fast disappearing from the data communications sector of computer science. A logical record is now referred to as a *message*; a physical record is now referred to as a *block* (second generation) or a *frame* (third and fourth generations). Data files residing on computers still have records, but the meaningful entities of data transmission are messages.

No. of fields	Field ID	Length of field	Contents of 1st field	Field ID	Length	Contents of 2nd field

FIGURE 10-1. Record Containing Its Own Parameters (Field ID's and Length Counters)

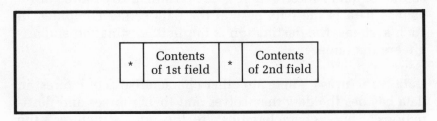

FIGURE 10-2. Record Containing Its Own Parameters (Field Separators)

Message Control Information The type of information that describes the payload data contained within a communication is called *message control information*. Such information includes the following:

- Identification of the beginning, middle, and end of data
- Data mode (binary or binary coded decimal, BCD)
- Character mode (ASCII, EBCDIC, for example)
- Application for which the data are intended
- Geographic destination, if not included within application
- Source of the data
- Priority of the data
- Security codes
- Integrity codes

Elements of Message Control Beginnings, intermediate portions, and ends of data are important because the data of a message may be strung out (fragmented) over several physical transmissions or crowded (concatenated) into one physical transmission with several other messages, even messages intended for other destinations. Figure 10-3 gives examples of fragmentation and concatenation. The other elements of control information are usually found in a *header* portion of a message as distinct from the *text* or data portion (see Figure 10-4).

The data mode is required in a system that handles more than one mode. This flag enables the terminal or application to correctly interpret the data presented to it. Character mode is similarly needed in networks that mix various types of terminals and computers so that payload data may be passed back and forth among them. Note that a character mode flag is not necessary for intermediate computers between the source terminal and the destination. These computers will not make conversions if the destination is clearly identified in a portion of the transmission independent of character mode.

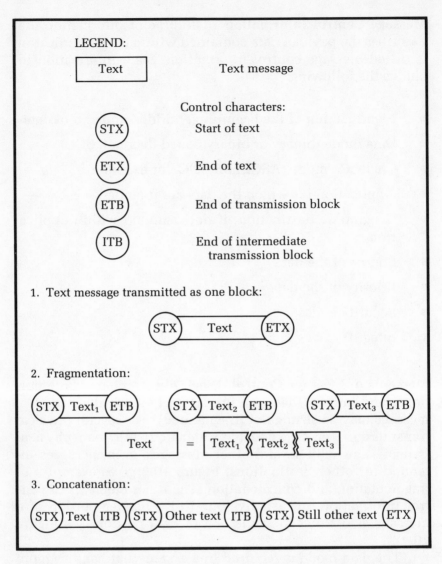

FIGURE 10-3. Examples of Fragmentation and Concatenation Using IBM's Binary Synchronous Communications (BSC) Protocol

The destination is obviously needed in those message-switching systems where it is not implicit in the data content of the message. In multiple-application data centers it is not enough to know and display in message control information

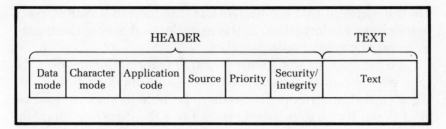

FIGURE 10-4.   Header and Text Portions of a Message

the address of the target computer. Message control must also address the application for which the message is intended.

In many systems it is assumed that a reply will be sent to the originator. If the source is not implicit in the data being transmitted or if such information is not available to switching software, then the source must be included in message control information.

Priority of information is usually a code assigned by the originator to indicate what price he or she is willing to pay for special treatment. Such information usually cannot be deduced from the data content and must be explicitly included as control information.

Security codes are affixed to data primarily for the purpose of preventing the system from transmitting the data to the wrong application or destination.

Integrity codes are mathematical patterns generated by software (or hardware, of course) to guard against transmission errors by identifying the results of such errors.

Thus we see that message control information is information about payload data. Message control information is usually contained in the same transmission as the payload data that it controls, but some messages contain control information that simply prepares the way or inquires about those messages that do contain payload data.

Network Control Information   Unlike payload data and message control information, network control information has very little to do with the applications for which the network has been constructed. Payload and message control information are the material that the network is intended to transmit. Network control information is the material that makes the transmission of payload data possible.

A network needs to interchange information among its members about its general well-being and the condition of its lines (links) and nodes. It needs to be able to start up and to shut down its various members and to substitute one member for another. A network must be able to choose times and routes for messages and to pass along to all components concerned the routing decisions that have been made.

The Principle of Reconfiguration For complete flexibility in dealing with its workload within its physical environment, the network must be able to dissociate its logical configuration from its physical configuration. The network adapts itself to the dynamic changes in its workload and its physical condition by making corresponding changes in its logical configuration. In hierarchical and star-shaped networks, however, there is only a limited amount of reconfiguration possible. Reconfiguration is restricted to deleting and restoring links or nodes. There is only one path from any one terminal to any other—that is, there is a unique sequence of nodes from a given source to a given destination. The reconfiguration options are thus:

- Disconnect the path
- Reconnect the path

Reconfiguration in Distributed Networks In distributed networks, however, there is greater flexibility for reconfiguration. In such networks, between any one source and any one destination there are many paths. Reconfiguration options, then, consist of:

- Deleting a link or node
- Restoring a link or node
- Assigning a particular path between two nodes
- Exchanging one path for another

In distributed networks with centralized control, a reconfiguration is accomplished by the control computer's sending a network control message to every node that is affected by the reconfiguration. Centralized control networks are of two types—those where every node has full information about the network and those where the nodes have information only about their immediate neighbors. In the first case, every node is affected by reconfiguration, so every node is notified. In the second case, the network control information is sent only to those nodes that are being reconfigured or to their immediate neighbors.

In distributed networks without centralized control, a reconfiguration occurs ad hoc as the result of some localized situation. The node involved may communicate the change in an explicit fashion to its neighbors, or it may be unable to communicate, in which case its neighbors may deduce the change. This is the way ARPAnet works. In such a case, distant nodes may not be informed about the change directly but may gradually become aware of it because of changes in the behavior of payload message traffic through that part of the system.

Other logical reconfiguration options are common to both classes of networks. They include renaming terminals (substitute routing) and exchanging one terminal's name with another's (alternate routing).

SUMMARY

This chapter shows that payload data is not sufficient in modern systems for network management purposes or even for all applications requirements. It has introduced the concept of meta information—information about payload data. It shows how metadata must use the very same network transmission functions and facilities as payload data and must be handled in just the same ways. The discussion of reconfiguration has shown what new functions can be developed to take advantage of metadata.

REFERENCES

Miscellaneous Data Communications Topics

Green, P. E., Jr., and Lucky, R. W., eds. *Computer Communications*. IEEE Press, 1974.

Martin, J. T. *Future Developments in Telecommunications*. New York: Prentice-Hall, Inc., 1970.

Martin, J. T., and Norman, A. *The Computerized Society*. New York: Prentice-Hall, Inc., 1970.

11

Meta-communications—Network Control and Error Recovery

The data communications environment is not the world of syntactic and deterministic logic that exists inside the CPU. Instead, the data communications environment is a world of statistical and random behavior. Consequently, when we move information from place to place in a network, we must use more than the data structures that contain the information or payload data that we want to move. We must also use structures that permit us to distinguish and recover from faults in the data. I call these structures metacommunications. Control information in metacommunications is contained in the structures themselves, and both sender and receiver can interpret them.

In this chapter, we discuss these new structures—error recovery data structures. Then we show how these structures are used for the following network control activities: monitoring, allocating, reclaiming, and recovering.

Error Recovery Data Structures   The data structures of network control range from the obvious, such as the transmitted

143

character or block, to the subtle, such as the network control functions. Figure 11-1 shows communications data structures for error recovery of these elements.

Graphic Examples Figure 11-2 shows a typical character error recovery data structure. Note that the parity bit may be used for error detection, leading to error recovery by means of retransmission, when:

- Characters are transmitted singly, as in asynchronous transmission

- Characters transmitted as a block preserve their individual parities, as in isosynchronous transmission where both individual character and group parity structures are used

Figure 11-3 shows a block error recovery data structure for binary synchronous communication (BSC), IBM's synchronous protocol developed in the 1960's. The block check character (BCC) indicates a longitudinal record check for ASCII and a cyclic redundancy check (CRC) for EBCDIC. The BCC is used for error detection and causes retransmission in this kind of system.

Object of Error Recovery	Error Recovery Data Structure
(1) Character	(1) Parity bits
(2) Block or frame	(2) Cyclic redundancy check (CRC) or parity bits
(3) Message	(3) Headers, trailers, block/ frame counts
(4) Function	(4) Protocol
(5) Device	(5) Status register
(6) System	(6) Logical organization

FIGURE 11-1. Error Recovery Data Structures

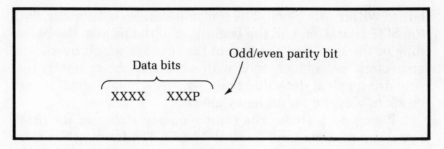

FIGURE 11-2. ASCII Character Error Recovery Data Structure

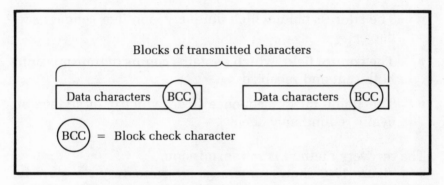

FIGURE 11-3. Block Error Recovery Structure for Binary Synchronous Communication (BSC)

Figure 11-4 shows a message error recovery structure for a binary synchronous communication system. Here, the messages optionally begin with a header, which may or may not be fully contained within one block. Similarly, the text may stretch over more than one block or several texts may be con-

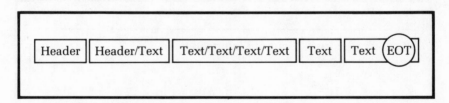

FIGURE 11-4. BSC Message Error Recovery Structure

tained within one block. The transmission ends, however, with the EOT character, and the beginning of the header, the beginning of the text, and the end of the text are set off by special characters. Each block ends with a block check character that contains an error detection code—either a longitudinal record check or a cyclic redundancy check.

Figure 11-5 shows the error recovery structure for IBM's Synchronous Data Link Control (SDLC). The framing bits mark the beginning and ending of a data transmission and serve for timing corrections as well. The other error detection/recovery substructures shown here include:

- The address field, which uniquely identifies sender or receiver

- The control field, which contains counts of transmissions both sent and received

- The frame check sequence (fcs), which is a sixteen-bit cyclic redundancy check

The recovery method is retransmission.

Figure 11-6 shows a message error recovery structure for the ARPAnet.

The Hierarchy of These Data Structures   There are also data structures in data communications functions. These structures are the protocol through which the functions communicate. This communication includes such things as positive and negative acknowledgment of messages. The first four error recovery data structures—those for characters, frames, messages,

Framing	Address	Control	Information	Frame check sequence	Framing

FIGURE 11-5.   IBM's Synchronous Data Link Control (SDLC) Error Recovery Data Structure

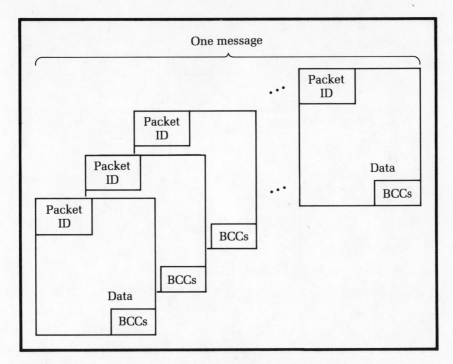

FIGURE 11-6. ARPAnet Message Error Recovery Data Structure

and functions—make up a nested set of data structures (see Figure 11-7).

The data structure for error recovery of a device is reflected in the status register that is obtained from the hardware controller before and after the device is activated. The device may be a communications line. It may also be a magnetic disc, an operator's console, or a line printer.

Network Error Recovery Data Structures The error recovery data structure of a system is the logical organization of that system. For example, in a star-shaped or hierarchical network, error recovery is implemented through a central processor that is said to have the complete intelligence of the network. In a distributed network, error control responsibility lies with individual processors, which make judgments about the activities of the other processors and are responsible for communicating their decisions to the other processors.

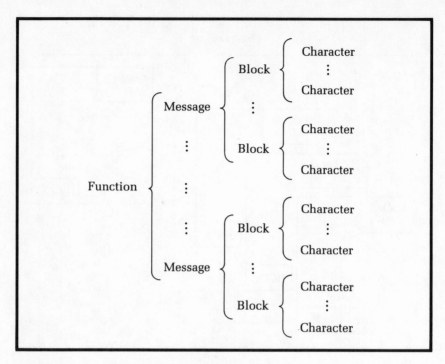

FIGURE 11-7. Nested Error Recovery Data Structures

In a network, error recovery may also be partially contained within each processor; for instance, each has the ability to correct an individual message. Error recovery may also exist in the form of downline loading of modules that are sent to malfunctioning processors within the network (see Figure 11-8).

Network Control

Data communications software uses the structures of the preceding section to deduce information about the status of the entire network and of its separate entities such as terminals and data links. Network control also uses the information contained within the structures to draw conclusions about the quality of individual transmissions and to decide what action should be taken with all transmissions. The software activities of network control are the following:

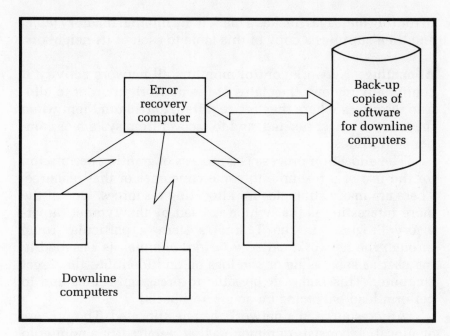

FIGURE 11-8. Configuration for Downline Loading Error Recovery

- Monitoring
- Allocating
- Reclaiming
- Recovering

Monitoring The network control software must know what is happening in the network. It obtains the required information in two ways:

- By direct inquiry (as in IBM's System Network Architecture, SNA)
- By indirect inference (as in the ARPAnet)

The structure used by the ARPAnet is maintained internally in each of the interface message processors (IMP's). This table is continually updated by the IMP. The IMP receives a status message from each of its neighbor IMP's once every two seconds; it compares this information with its own experience in routing messages, makes a mark in its internal memory table, and then supplies a copy of this table to each of its neighbors.

Allocating   Network control monitors all network activity. It continually reviews the status of the network in order to allocate resources where they are required, to reclaim them when they are no longer needed, and to recover from system or component failures.

The allocation process is a process of granting permission for the use of a resource to some consumer of that resource. There are many strategies for allocating resources. One of the more interesting is that which is used by the Tymnet Supervisory Program. In the Tymnet system, a particular route through the network, called a *virtual channel*, is assigned to the user as soon as he or she logs on and identifies the target computer. This makes it possible to preassign routes and to perform load balancing on an a priori basis.

Any resource in a network may be allocated. The process of allocating consists of removing that resource, or a pointer to that resource, from one queue and placing the pointer into another queue (see Figure 11-9).

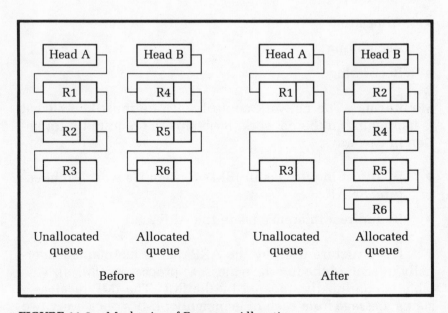

FIGURE 11-9.   Mechanics of Resource Allocation

Reclaiming The reclaiming process uses the same mechanical process as allocation, but it works in the opposite sequence. The normal termination of the use of any resource results in a direct call to the resource reclaiming subfunction of network control. An unusual termination results in an indirect call. Figures 11-10, 11-11, and 11-12 show the control sequences for allocation and reclaiming.

Recovering Network control uses several different means to recover from system or network failure. These means include the following:

- Block, frame, or message *recovery* through parity error detection and retransmission or forward error correction (FEC)

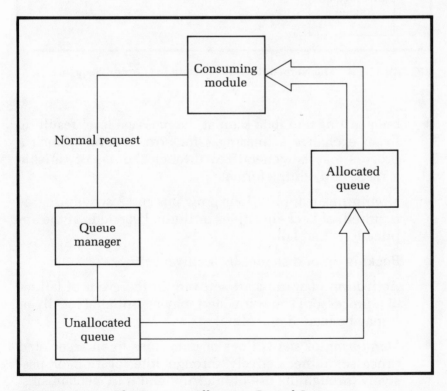

FIGURE 11-10. The Resource Allocation Control Sequence

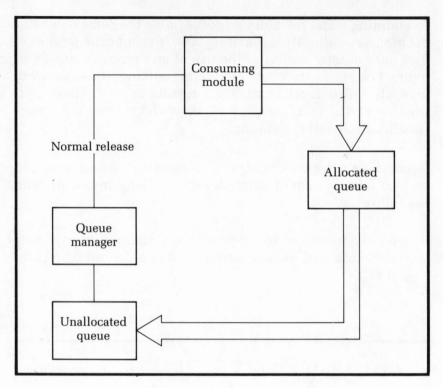

FIGURE 11-11. The Normal Resource Reclaiming Control Sequence

- Data *editing* and data *scan* at the message level resulting in an exchange of messages for error recovery (Such a process may be generalized through the use of variable screens and editing formats.)

- *Monitoring* of applications programs and rescheduling, as required, of back-up copies or limited versions of the applications that fail

- *Backing up* of disc files by archival software

- *Activation* of warm-start software in the event of failure of a processor (The warm start may be initiated locally or it may be loaded downline)

- *Monitoring* of status lines or data lines to an associated processor either actively through interrogation or passively through the use of interrupt and trap mechanisms

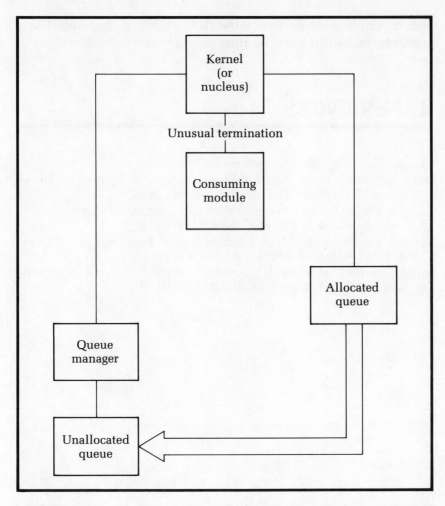

FIGURE 11-12. The Unusual Termination Resource Reclaiming Control Sequence

SUMMARY

This chapter continues the discussion of meta information. It looks at the data structures that contain meta information and shows how they are used in monitoring network performance and in implementing the network resource management operations—allocation, reclaiming, and recovery.

REFERENCES

General Computer Science References

Halstead, Maurice H. *Machine-Independent Computer Programming*. Washington, D. C.: Spartan Books, 1962.

Jordain, Philip B., and Breslau, Michael. *Condensed Computer Encyclopedia*. St. Louis: McGraw-Hill, 1969.

Ralston, Anthony, and Meek, Chester, L., eds. *Encyclopedia of Computer Science*. New York: Petrocelli/Charter, 1976.

Sippl, Charles J., and Sippl, Charles P. *Computer Science Dictionary and Handbook*. New York: Bobbs-Merrill, 1972.

CONCLUDING NOTES

I have written this book with the intention of taking some of the mystery out of data communications software. I feel that most programmers who start to do data communications work have had to dive right into the middle of the technology; no one took the time to explain to them why we have to provide the elements we put into data communications systems.

As I got deeper into the work, I found that some of the most important concepts in the field lacked vigorous definition. By defining these concepts as I have, I hope that I am not merely adding to an already long list of terms, but that I have been at least modestly successful in organizing and explaining what is generally known about data communications. For me, formalizing data communications is only a secondary aim. I am primarily interested in just explaining software and simplifying wherever I can. I hope I have been more successful there. Meanwhile, the formalization still needs to be done.

The standards groups are hard at work on developing standards, but their focus seems limited at present to protocols. Yet, until terminology and concepts have been formalized, I feel that networks will continue to be developed on an ad hoc basis with essentially incompatible architectures.

It is my hope that the industry will turn to this task of formalization soon. It should result in faster learning time, greater economies in system and network development costs, and more reliable data communications software that is easier to maintain.

INDEX

157

National Institute of Health's
MEDLINE, 130
Natural rhythm, 96
Negative acknowledgment, 146
Network, 15
Network application(s), 13, 133
Network architecture(s), 7, 15, 16
Network configuration control,
107
Network control, 33, 39, 41–43,
141, 143–144, 148–152
Network control information, 134,
139–140
Network management, 86, 99,
104–107
Network-oriented
communications, 33
Network-oriented protocols, 38
Network throughput, 15
New York Times Infobank, 130
Noise, 37

Off-track betting, 14
On-line data entry, 2
Online update, 99, 130–132
Operating system, 13
Operating system interface, 114
Organization, administrative, 62
Organization, geographic, 62
Organization, temporal, 62
Output channel, 67
Output writer, 122

Packaging requirements, 94
Packet switching, 15
Paper tape, 2
Parity bit, 76
Parity checking, 58
Parity error, 151
Passbook accounting, 99
Path(s), 104–105
Payload, 26, 124, 139
Payload data, 26, 28, 95, 135, 137,
139, 141
Payload message(s), 30, 135
Polling, 107
Port, 10
Presentation control, 38
Primary channel, 49, 59
Priority, 96, 137, 139

Private line, 24
Privileged instructions, 13
Probes, 108
Process control, 43
Programs, 2
Program control, 22
Program control information, 32
Program-controlled data transfer,
57
Program-to-program data, 32
Programmer, applications, 12, 13
Programmer, systems, 13
Protocol(s), 5, 37–39, 41–42, 44,
55, 61, 146
Protocols, hardware, 44
Protocol, level(s) of, 16, 28
Protocols, link, 108
Protocols, software, 5, 59, 61, 65
Punched cards, 2
Purging rhythm, 96
Pushdown stack, 68

QTAM, 12
Queue, buffer, 80, 119
Queue, command processor's, 126
Queue, first-time-execution, 126
Queue handler, 130
Queue, in-core, 126
Queue management, 95–96, 106,
120, 128, 130
Queue manager(s), 97, 102, 120,
126, 130
Queue, message, 119
Queueing, 13, 102
Queueing, disk, 120

Reader, 121
Real time, 32, 69, 127–128
Realtime clock, 70
Real-time transmission, 2
Receive timing, 52
Reclaiming, 149, 151, 154
Reconfiguration, 140–141
Record, 136
Recovering, 149, 151, 154
Recovery, 15
Reentrancy, 99, 129
Reentrant, 129, 132
Reentrant code, 129